Transcend and Transform

Transcend and Transform

An Introduction to Conflict Work

Johan Galtung

Paradigm Publishers

BOULDER

Published in the United States by Paradigm Publishers
3360 Mitchell Lane, Boulder, Colorado 80301 USA.

Paradigm Publishers is the trade name of Birkenkamp & Company, LLC, Dean Birkenkamp, President and Publisher.

First published in the United Kingdom by Pluto Press
345 Archway Road, London N6 5AA

Library of Congress Cataloging in Publication Data has been applied for.

ISBN 1–59451–062–8 (hbk.: alk. paper)
ISBN 1–59451–063–6 (pbk.: alk. paper)

Printed and bound in the European Union on acid-free paper that meets the standards of the American National Standard for Permanence of Paper for Printed Library Materials.

09   08   07   06   05   04
5   4   3   2   1

Contents

Preface

The author has been a mediator, adviser and participant in a series of conflicts around the world for more than 40 years, from everyday life conflicts to the geopolitical level. These experiences have been used in conflict training, also around the world. This is an effort to present something of that training in the shape of a book, with 40 cases, 'from everyday life to the geopolitical'.

Conflicts do not exist at higher or lower levels. All conflicts are born equal and have the same right to be processed, with transcendence ('going beyond') and transformation, so that the parties can live with them. Geopolitical conflicts are not on a 'higher level' because statesmen and diplomats have high social status. All conflicts are equal: they are deeply serious for everybody concerned. Conflicts are not a game to be won or lost, but are often a struggle to survive, for well-being, freedom, identity – all basic human needs.

No special advanced knowledge is needed to read this book. All that is required is that the reader does a little work. Close the book when the conflict has been formulated and think through what you would have advised. What would you have said, what would you have done? Then read on. As a standard exercise: find another example for yourself and think it through.

First, a few words about how these examples are used in training around the world by the mediation organisation TRANSCEND (www.transcend.org). A room, five dialogue tables in a semicircle with six people seated at each. Nobody has their back to the course instructor, who stands in the centre of the circle, with a flip chart. He/she sketches a conflict: who are the parties, what are their goals, where are the incompatibilities ('contradictions')? Then the task is put to all the tables: what would you suggest? Or select three from any number of tables.

Five – ten – fifteen minutes of dialogue, with each table appointing a spokesperson. The proposals are presented, written up, there is discussion, comments. It has been done this way in many languages in a score of places around the world. But in addition to that, TRANSCEND Peace University (TPU) is on-line (www.transcend. org/tpu) offering several courses. Once again the TPU participants are divided into dialogue groups, across continents, they appoint one person to write, and the job rotates. Their common basic texts are *Searching for Peace* (London: Pluto Press, 2nd edition 2002) and *Peace by Peaceful Means* (London: Sage, 1998). A small group in which everybody has a chance to talk can draw on more experience and creativity than is possible for a single individual.

This book can also be read by a study group which discusses every case, not necessarily ending in a consensus among themselves or with the author. But it comes with a guarantee: the participants will learn a lot!

The chapters in this book bear the names of the days of the week, thus reflecting more or less what happens in an on-site course of one week's duration. Spend seven days on the book, alone or in a group/ study circle/colloquium. The book draws more on how much you have lived than on how much you have read, and gives you a basis, as an amateur or as a professional, for conflict work, to help others and yourself – an introduction to elementary conflict hygiene.

The book is based on real, not imagined conflicts, and most of it draws on my experience as a usually invited mediator. Monday is devoted to conflicts within and between persons (micro); Tuesday to conflicts within a society (meso); Wednesday to conflict among states and among nations (macro) and Thursday to conflicts among regions and civilisations (mega). *Micro – Meso – Macro – Mega*, from the close to the distant. Friday and Saturday are devoted to other themes the four levels have in common. And Sunday is an overview and conclusion.

Good luck! Think fruitful, optimistic thoughts and dream rich dreams, inspired by a diagram you will read quite a lot about:

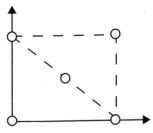

Johan Galtung
Kyoto/Alfaz
April 2001/January 2004

Introduction

Dear reader, all you need is a strip of paper, say 20 cm long and 2 cm wide, and a pencil. At the head of the strip you write A, and at the bottom, but on the other side, you write B. And then recite two wishes over and over again so that in the end you *feel* them:

I want a line, not necessarily a straight one, that connects A and B.
The line mustn't cross over the edge of the strip.

Your problem takes the form of a contradiction between two goals. You can draw a line from A to B, but it will cross over the edge even if you join the ends so that the strip takes the form of a doughnut: A and B will still be on opposite sides. You can avoid crossing over the edge, but in that case you don't get from A to B. You can attempt a compromise, going from A almost to the edge, and then, turning the strip over, almost from the edge to B. But in that case you are cheating, as the line does not join up. You can get angry and refuse to draw a line (India), bomb the book (the USA), skip this page, reproach the author as arrogant (Norway) – in short, you can give up. Or you can read on, unless you are one of those who know about the Möbius strip or have that talent conflict workers need more than anyone else: imagination and creativity. You hold the strip in one hand and turn one end over before you join the two ends. A and B are now on the same side – in fact, everything is on the same side. The contradiction has been transcended; it no longer exists. A twist, a transformed doughnut, and the problem is solved.

But this isn't a conflict! Well, the roots of a conflict are here: contradiction. Imagine now that one side of you says 'Let's cross over the edge!', while another side says 'It's not that important that the line joins up!', a third says 'Compromise!' a fourth: 'It's a ridiculous problem, we have more important things to do!' That's four ways to avoid the challenge. But then a fifth says, let us explore with August Möbius (after whom the strip is named) the centrepiece of any transcendence: *both/and* (even with a twist).

Now we reach the nub of this book. Simple, but it is going to become more complicated as we proceed. What is important is to get a grip on the underlying ideas rather than to 'see' the solution immediately.

But first, a few words about the goals and parties in a conflict. Goals can be positive or negative, something to be pursued or something to be avoided. *Goals* and *life* – living beings, humans and animals, plants and micro-organisms, you and I – are inseparable. Only what is living has a goal. Without a goal life ceases to exist. One of the last goals of a dying human may be goallessness itself, eternal rest. Goals nag at us. There is no limit to the activity we undertake in order to achieve or satisfy our goals.

Where there are goals there will also often be contradictions within the same organism or between them; here and now, here or there, now or later. 'There are human beings without contradictions. They are called corpses', the Chinese say. Life, goal and contradiction are inseparable. 'Conflict prevention', preventing conflicts, is meaningless. But 'violence prevention', preventing violence, is extremely meaningful and beneficial. This book is intended as a contribution to that.

If we say that a mountain has as its goal to surge upwards, then we attribute life to that mountain. 'Oslo' and 'Norway' do not have goals, they are organisations, not organisms. But mayors, prime ministers and the chief executive officers of corporations have goals. They have life.

When an individual or group pronounces its position on the goals of cities or states they often use the word 'interests'. In doing so they are indicating that these are not randomly chosen goals from a catalogue of goals, but something deeply anchored in the organisation, in its very foundations.

But interests are often the badly concealed formulations of the goals of the leaders, for instance that a country, town, organisation should be bigger and more powerful. Maybe they think this will make them big and powerful too.

Some goals take priority over others because they are absolute, necessary conditions for the continued life of individual organisms. If they are not satisfied, life and human dignity cease to be possible. *Survival – well-being – freedom – identity* are basic needs. They are deeper than values, above values. We can choose our values, and choice is part of our freedom. Values become part of our identity; to have precisely those values is itself valued. But basic needs are different. You don't choose your basic needs; basic needs choose you. It is their satisfaction that makes you possible. If you negotiate away your own or others' basic needs, you are sentencing yourself or others to a life unworthy of human beings. You are exercising violence. Negotiation is possible where goals and values are concerned, but not with basic needs. Basic needs have to be respected; they are non-negotiable.

In a sense satisfaction of basic needs is the only legitimate, valid interest for 'Norway', 'Oslo', the 'organisation of businesses'. Other 'interests', such as power and size, do not necessarily have to be the means of satisfying basic needs. But what we can ask from them is that they do not insult our basic needs. If they do, things begin to get serious. *Insulting basic needs – that is violence.*

Basic needs regulate the relation between you and your environment; what goes in and out of the eight openings of the human *body* (remember the skin!) Who controls that? You, or somebody else? This is not only a question of the body, but also of the *soul*, as a storehouse of perceived impressions and emotions, sometimes released in expressions.

And then there is the *spirit*, the ability to reflect on how body and soul have been deeply *programmed,* and how to change the programme. We do not attribute this capacity to animals, plants and micro-organisms, but regard them as programmed towards the very end, by 'instincts'. Basic needs cannot be negotiated away. We insult the needs of animals and plants by using them, even exterminating them. Harmony = mutual basic need satisfaction is something we have only with our pets.

Concrete examples will now lead us towards concepts and theories of conflict. We will start with conflicts within individuals (dilemmas) and between individuals (disputes). You will recognise them. This also applies to conflicts between groups such as between genders, classes, races. But try to be equally concerned with conflicts between states and nations, regions and civilisations. You read, listen, see them in the media, presented as a game between states and between corporations. But they concern you, and all readers, listeners, viewers. Democracy calls for *your* interest and knowledge. This is the message from the major popular revolts of our time, the peace movement and the Porto Alegre movement, against death and misery, against the power games of states and corporations. The movements are a shock to those who negotiate away the basic needs of millions. But today the contradictions between state/capital and the common people are being globalised and acted out at the mega-level, between regions, between civilisations.

Let us hold on to the central point in a conflict. There are goals that cannot be satisfied. They are blocked. In other words, there is *frustration*. That is bad enough. But *conflict* goes one step further.

There are at least two goals. But one obstructs the other and is carried by some Other. The relationship with a goal becomes a relationship with that Other. He may even be a part of ourselves, and in that case we can talk about a dilemma. As Goethe said, 'There are two souls in my breast.' 'Why only two?' a Frenchman retorted.

The relationship will then quickly be filled with strong emotions ranging from hatred to apathy, and contempt for one's own betrayal if a goal is abandoned or one simply escapes. The brain in the stomach communicates with diarrhoea and vomiting, with feeling faint, the twisting of the guts. You are seething. Hands that you can use to caress the one you love are clenched into fists. Colour drains from your face. The brain in your head is decoupled when you need it more than ever in order to process large quantities of facts and goals towards a sustainable solution that can be accepted and sustained.

Conflict touches everything in us, our feelings, our thoughts. Conflicts demand of us everything we have to offer. If not, our emotions will easily be expressed as violence, insulting the basic needs of others, as verbal violence, physical violence, or both.

In this book, 40 cases from real life will be explored. But let us start with the good old orange example, written up and published as a fable, *A Flying Orange Tells Its Tale*, and illustrated by Andreas Galtung.

I once used it in London at a conference on bullying between children, their parents and their teachers. There were ten tables, with two people at each table, and one orange on each table. We started with the youngest and proceeded to the oldest to see how they viewed the 'situation'. The word 'conflict' was deliberately avoided. The first person to pronounce herself was an eight-year-old girl, the best student in England in her class that year. 'I would peel the orange,' she said, 'and count the number of slices. If the number is even, I would divide by two – and then he can choose. If the number is odd, I would also divide by two and carefully divide the remaining slice into two bits.'

Totally correct, but as uncreative as those who wanted to make the division with a knife – usually men; women are more oriented towards peeling – and then slurping one half each. Others would squeeze the juice and divide it equally between two glasses. A good basis for teaching mathematics, physics and chemistry.

Then there were those who wanted to toss a coin and those who said, 'I would buy the orange!' Or the boy who wanted to fight for it. But that was the wrong answer. We wanted outcomes both parties could accept, a sustainable way into the future, with no afterthought of revenge and/or revanche.

After a while, more creative proposals emerged. Some children wanted to play with the orange. Two girls from India simply wanted to look at it, the orange was so beautiful, 'to look together is to share it'. Then there were those who wanted to make cups out of the peel, use the peel to make cakes that could be sold, auctioned or used in a lottery. And finally there were those who wanted to plant the pips and reap the harvest in 20 years. At least 16 qualitatively different outcomes, but very few were able to arrive at more than six or seven.

The broader the spectrum of solutions, the more alternatives there are to violence. And this is the major point if we are to prevent conflict sliding into violence: use the energy conflict generates to arrive at creative solutions.

Monday: Micro-Conflicts Within and Between Persons

In a sense it's strange that humanity didn't turn out even worse.

That our goals are sometimes unrealistic and that we have to live with frustration is bad enough. But this, of course, is the art of living, to hold the bow so high that the arrow flies a long distance and hits the mark, but not so high that the arrow falls short of the goal or the bowstring snaps.

Then there is this thing about incompatible goals. What is my goal as a human being? Is it wealth, becoming rich in terms of the things I *have*, or a rich inner life in the sense of what I *am*? Both, but what if they stand in each other's way? Should I be kind and help my competitor, or ambitious and beat him? Both, but how? Behind such choices there are principles that together make up our philosophy of life. Some can stand the light of day better than others. It is not a bad idea to take a sheet of paper and write at its head 'My Philosophy of Life'. Fill the sheet, look it in the eye. How do you react to an exercise like this? Perhaps there are at least two souls in your breast, each with its own philosophy of life? If you try to repress one of them it can damage your mental health. It's better to see if you can modify, moderate, mediate, bridge the gap between them.

But what about the goals that bring us into struggle with others? Tell me how you react in a conflict and I can tell you a lot about how much peace there is inside you. A volcanic eruption, 'talking it over', can clear the air. But what about him or her, the victim of the eruption? If your 'choleric personality' becomes a habit, it can add considerably to the problems of both of you.

So take it easy, let nothing show on the outside, not even in the depth of your soul, and people will love you because you never challenge them. But if that becomes a habit, then your 'sanguine, imperturbable personality' can become a problem for you yourself. Disappointment associated with the unrealised goal, or your resentment, or whatever stood in the way can lead to ugly reactions within you and towards others. You can easily end up permanently 'offended'.

Your conflict style can express an offence around which you have constructed your life rather than process it; that's reached epidemic proportions in introverted cultures like the Norwegian and Japanese. The choleric, the volcanic one, can avoid this when he feels that 'justice is being served' and he can draw on his own eruptions as a source of happiness. But in doing so he is also exploiting those who are the victims of his eruptions.

Conflict styles cover more than the choleric and sanguine personalities though. These are only two ways of handling emotions, frozen into personal strategies for survival in conflict. What they have in common is an inability to handle the contradiction itself, the root of the conflict. The styles are on the surface of the conflict, in our body language, in what we say, verbal violence and, in more extreme cases, in what we do, physical violence. The high temperature in the choleric, and the low temperature in the sanguine, personality are two versions of defeat relative to the major task: taking on the challenge, solving the conflict, bridging the contradiction.

This calls for another resource we all have, our intellectual capacity. Conflicts can be analysed, they can be understood. Conflicts address everything in us, our emotions, thoughts and more. So we have to try to address them and not only give in to our emotions. We need preventive intellectual work before emotions take over and the gut brain prevails over the head brain, in the high-level, mass murder temperature as in Croatia and Bosnia, or in the low-level temperature as in the bad decisions behind the politics in Bosnia (see Wednesday, Yugoslavia).

What this book offers is an intellectual technique for that kind of preventive work in conflicts at all levels of organisation. Conflict and peace research are spanning the whole field and are not, as some people seem to believe, some kind of left-wing approach to foreign policy. So let us start where people feel most at home, with a simple example from daily life.

THE FLYING COUPLE

A couple, a man and woman, often travel long distances by plane, ten-, twelve-hour trips. They like to sit next to each other, to be able to have a drink, talk about how horrible airline food is, how crazy the world is. About everything.

But they have a problem – ten hours is quite a long time. Sometimes they want to stretch their legs or go to the toilet. This is easier if you have an aisle seat, you don't have to apologise to your neighbour. But who is going to have that aisle seat?

Man:	It has to be me. Everyone knows that men, particularly when they are getting on a bit, have to go to the toilet more frequently.
Woman:	I thought there was something known as courtesy in this world, that men could be gallant, that there could be more chivalry, that we could be given a tiny advantage –
Man:	Ha! So that we can exploit you even more, socially, economically?
Woman:	No, no, not like that. But don't you men always get the aisle seats? And why should we always be the ones to apologise?
Conflict Worker:	Well, this is a conflict. A 'conflict is a contradiction between goals', in this case 'aisle seat for the man' and 'aisle seat for the woman'. The parties are the man and the woman, the goals are aisle seats and there is a contradiction because there is only one aisle seat and they want to sit next to each other. Can you suggest any solutions?
Man:	We could change seats. Midway. Or every other trip.
Woman:	I don't think that solves the problem. There will still be a lot of getting up and down. In that case, I would rather give up flying.
Man and Woman in unison, suddenly:	Unless we sit on both sides of the aisle! A little distance, but contact, a drink, and –
Woman:	And perhaps a little less about the insanity of the world?
Man:	And perhaps a little less about the abominable airline food!
Conflict Worker:	You have found the both/and: but very many people are too tied to the notion of 'sitting next to each other' to look across the aisle and try both aisle seats rather than having an aisle seat every second trip, or taking fewer flights. In other words, the trick is to escape from that thought prison!

THE DRESS

A Mother's Story: I am 43 years old. Twenty-five years ago I graduated from high school and tonight we are having a reunion to celebrate. I am looking forward to it – and I am apprehensive. I will put on a dress which is clearly too young for me. It's a bit tight, a bit short. I have my doubts about it. But then I have a daughter who is 18 years old like I was when I graduated. I have brought her up as well as I could to focus on two important goals in life: Be *considerate*! Be *honest*!

So I put on the dress, knock and enter her room. There she is, beautiful I think, preparing for an oral exam. She knows that this is an important day for me. I take a few steps forward, stop, watching her with spaniel eyes begging for a little tenderness. And then I say quietly but clearly 'What do you think?'

Conflict Worker: Well, what is your advice? Remember, the answer has to be both considerate *and* honest, not one or the other. And you have to reply quickly. You have just five seconds. If you hesitate, then a nervous mother will easily resort to tears. What's wrong with the dress?! With me?!

A Daughter's Story: And then mother comes in as I am sitting learning all those things by heart. She is a wonderful mother, a good mother, but a little insecure. And she wanted me to say something about her dress which actually would have suited me much better. What am I supposed to say? It is easy enough to be considerate, 'Mum, you look wonderful, everything fits you!' but she is not stupid enough to rise to that bait. Or I can be honest and say 'Mum, are you really going to the reunion dressed up like you did at the time, how many years ago was it, 25?'

How I wish my mobile would ring so that I don't have to answer her! That would give me a little time to think it all through!

Daughter: Mum it's really nice, but perhaps not quite right for your – yes, I really like it, but on the other hand –

Mother: Is it 'age' you were going to say? If so, just say so!

Daughter: No, that's not what I mean, you always look so young! You look fine, but, on the other hand – how about a shawl?

Mother: Something's wrong, in other words. Just say so!

Daughter: Nothing's wrong, but perhaps the blue dress would be more appropriate?

Mother: The blue dress! It's so old-fashioned. So that's the kind of thing you think suits me! What kind of daughter do I have?!

Conflict Worker: What is happening here is an effort on the part of the daughter to solve the conflict. She is struggling with herself between honesty and consideration. The goals are eating away at her heart because she has internalised them. Betraying one of them is not without consequences for her, regardless of which one. A 'bad conscience' is that little arrow striking deep into our 'soul', whether that word stands for 'mind', or 'spirit', or both. She wants to avoid the whole situation and be saved by her mobile, and in so doing she will betray both goals. Then she tries a compromise, a mix of honest and considerate comments in the hope that together they will do the trick. She is brimming over with good intentions, but none of them satisfies her, or her mother.

Behind this dilemma there is a new conflict, one between mother and daughter. The daughter does her best to be honest without at the same time being inconsiderate, or to be considerate without at the same time being dishonest. But the mother simply does not like the answer. She becomes aggressive towards the daughter.

A concrete situation and a clear contradiction, conflict, between two goals. Is there a sentence that could transcend this contradiction, unifying the goals? With a twist as with the Möbius strip?

Some years ago this was the opening exercise in three courses for UN ambassadors in Geneva, in English, French and Spanish. They were supposed to find a phrase, a 'diplomatic answer', something diplomats presumably have as their speciality. But they were not able to do so.

Elsewhere, participants with much less formal education, mostly women, fold their hands and say something like this: 'Mum, you have such a fine personality, and I think the blue dress reflects your personality very well.'

Let us pay attention to three aspects of this answer, in addition to being *both* considerate *and* honest, provided the description of her personality is correct:

(1) The original contradiction between the mother and her dress, mirrored in the contradiction between consideration and honesty, is avoided. The sentence goes beyond, transcends, this contradiction. The catastrophic word 'but' in the daughter's 'but perhaps the blue dress', in other words negating the 'nothing is wrong' preceding it, is avoided. Instead the connecting word used is 'and'. *Avoid negatives.*

(2) The sentence is *future*-oriented, not oriented towards the present or the past.

(3) The sentence is *constructive*, with a clear directive for action.

If the mother accepts that sentence, then a sustainable solution to the problem of satisfying both goals has been reached.

Some talent is needed in order to reach such a formulation quickly, releasing a tense situation, without being devoid of content, as in the easygoing 'Mother, if the dress makes you feel good, then it's the right dress for you.'

How do you cultivate such a talent? You need:

- a very quick definition of the problem: to find a both/and answer;
- creativity to find an answer of that kind;
- the presentation of the solution as a proposal, not as an ultimatum.

And all that in less than five seconds in order to avoid the mother's 'What's the problem?!' Social experience from similar situations is useful, in other words, to have lived a full life, not only to have read many books, the usual problem of students who are too young and have often learnt more than they have experienced. What is needed is not only social intelligence but conventional intelligence in order to recognise a pattern, drawing on 'this reminds me of a problem I came across last week'. Before we proceed, let us pay attention to a *neither/nor*; neither considerate, nor honest, answers which will become quite important later:

Daughter: Mother, why don't we have lunch together tomorrow?

A conflict theory should offer more than merely an identification of badly needed capabilities. We also need a method that can be used for those who have not yet developed those abilities. We need a method that is systematic, not only a mapping of the outcomes a conflict can lead us into, but an overview of the processes that lead us to such outcomes. Thus, one of the diplomats suggested, and only partly as a joke, that what was needed was an internationally representative committee to find the formula that unties the knot. Fortunately, there are better, and less expensive, methods available!

In order to arrive at a map let us use the Cartesian coordinate system. This is indispensable and will appear several times in this book. The reader will be surprised how much can be squeezed out of that little diagram. But do check all the points in the diagram.

On the horizontal axis we put the degree of realisation (nothing – something – everything; or $0 - \frac{1}{2} -1$) for the goal *honesty*; on the vertical axis the same for the goal *consideration*. Within the diagram we can then plot all nine combinations. But we include only the five most important ones.

The basic diagram in the theory of conflict: Two incompatible goals, Five outcomes

Consideration	Everything	[2] (0,1)		[5] (1,1)
	Something		[4] ($\frac{1}{2}$,$\frac{1}{2}$)	
	Nothing	[3] (0,0)		[1] (1,0)
		Nothing	Something	Everything *Honesty*

The conflict consists in honesty and consideration apparently excluding each other. [5] is impossible. The solution lies in showing that with a little twist they no longer exclude each other. [5] becomes possible.

Let us now compare a number of formulations of these five points, all of them with a message, all of them with a story to tell.

NO.	POSITION		OUTCOME	PROCESS	SUM	JOB
[1]	1,0	Either-or	Victory	Struggle	1	1
[2]	0,1	Either-or	Victory	Struggle	1	1
[3]	0,0	Neither-nor	Withdrawal	Postponement	0	2
[4]	$\frac{1}{2}$,$\frac{1}{2}$	Half-half	Compromise	Negotiation	1	1
[5]	1,1	Both-and	Transcendence	Dialogue	2	0

[1] and [2] are clear. They are the same: one goal is realised, the other not. But we keep them apart. These are two different goals, or two different parties/persons with the same goal, like enjoying a single orange there on the table.

We have used words from the language of war such as 'victory' and 'struggle'. Victory points to the winner, and the winner presupposes a loser. But acceptability and sustainability are incompatible with having lost, unless the victory is seen as an expression of the will of God. The loser will often be thinking of nothing but revenge (harming/hurting the other party) and revanche (redistribution, but this time in favour of oneself). And the winner will easily acquire the very bad habit of wanting to win again. And then again. Victory is sweet. But victory can also be very expensive when loser and winner target each other and launch a vendetta through history. Thus, the USA was hit by 'terrorism' on 11 September. Could this have been the revenge/revanche for US 'victory' – a 'blowback'? If so, who was responsible?

We shall later show that both victory and struggle can have a clear, non-violent meaning and that they are indispensable as possible outcomes in a conflict under certain conditions.

[3] can mean several things. 'The time is not yet ripe' is a formula often used by politicians who themselves are not ripe or up to the problem, but waiting for 'time' to be certified as 'sufficiently ripe'.

But this could also be a way of acknowledging that we are all incapable at the present point in time. We are not 'sufficiently ripe', by which we mean 'mature'. Put the problem on hold, try to get some consensus around postponement, and then ...!

Neither/nor can also be a solution, as when the UN says neither/nor to two fighting parties and they themselves administer a territory like UNMIK in Kosovo. We can refer to this as *negative transcendence*, like the daughter's neither/nor in the form of 'having lunch together tomorrow', mentioned above.

[4] is the *compromise* so often praised: 'If both of them yield a little, they will find a solution', 'He is a man of compromise', 'The negotiations came to nothing because there was no will to compromise.'

In this book about the TRANSCEND method 'compromise' is not a positive word. Look it up in a Spanish or Italian dictionary and a double meaning becomes very clear: the will to yield, but also the will to sell oneself. Compromise is the comfort of the poor, he who knows so little about what can come out of a conflict that he believes compromise is the only alternative. What actually happens is a consensus about an outcome that satisfies nobody, often with both parties hoping that the other is at least equally dissatisfied, uniting round shared dissatisfaction, mutual congratulation, toasting that shared dissatisfaction.

[5] is *positive transcendence*, the key to transformation in the TRANSCEND method. Much is demanded. The task is to create a both/and where no such thing existed, not a 50/50 compromise, nor a victory, nor withdrawal – even though under some circumstances all of these other outcomes can enter the picture. Aim high, take the

jump. But that demands imagination, creativity. The negotiation table with the other party – who in addition is often an enemy who has killed several on one's own side – a couple of feet away is not the place. In other words, different approaches are needed to create a new reality.

There is a strong linkage between compromise and negotiations in many conflict cultures. We are not rejecting compromise and negotiation entirely, but see them as inferior to transcendence, going beyond, and dialogue.

The numbers under the headings SUM and JOB give us an idea of how far we have come and of how much work remains to be done for each outcome. It is like multiplying economic growth by economic distribution (from 0 for total inequality to 1 for total equality) in order to get an idea of where a country is located economically: 10 per cent growth with 0.5 in distribution yields 0.5, which could also mean 5 per cent growth with perfect distribution.

For the five points we get:

[1], [2] If we choose *struggle,* then we can arrive at victory, one goal satisfied, which means a job half done; with the risk that victory can be very expensive indeed. Victory can have in its wake revenge, revanche, arrogance.

[3] If we choose *postponement,* then no goal has been satisfied. A sum of 0 gives a remaining job of 2, maximum. Everything has been postponed. The conflict is still there and may be like a festering wound because goals have not been satisfied. An unsatisfied goal by definition leads to frustration, and if that goal is a basic need, this can overshadow everything else. Frustration then leads to aggression. The game of postponement can become like playing with fire. But the argument is not that frustration should be attended to in order to prevent violence. Rather it is that a basic need should be attended to, like the misery in the third world, whether 'we' are in danger or not.

Postponement, withdrawal, very rarely carry any sustainability. But negative transcendence can have some acceptability and sustainability because a new reality has been created.

[4] If we choose *compromise,* then the chance of acceptability is much higher. But sustainability will be temporary because the conflict is still there, glowing if not exploding because the contradictions have become less acute. Once again half the job remains to be done. But that is a different half from the one under [1] and [2]. [4] is at least symmetrical. Both are suffering.

[5] If we arrive at *positive transcendence*, then the job has been done. But here the problem may be that we have gone too far in our effort to 'go beyond'. The proposal may have been too creative to be understood, let alone accepted. The solution is too unusual.

Let us return to the dress scenario. It is easy to formulate an honest answer or a considerate answer. But something that is both honest and considerate does not arrive by itself. Somewhere the formulation is blocked. But then there is a jump. The block or hurdle is transcended with 'Mum, you have such a fine personality and the blue dress reflects that personality very well.' The daughter's conflict between being honest and considerate has encountered its both/and by simply jumping over the whole problem of the tight dress, bringing in another criterion and another dress. And in doing so she has transformed the whole conflict.

But that does not come with a guarantee that the solution of the mother's conflict between 'I am still young' and 'The dress does not quite fit me' has been accepted by her in a sustainable way beyond the moment of acceptance. Is she really going to try the blue dress? And will it really fit her? There could be problems with the blue dress too. And the mother could have deeper problems. Perhaps what she wants from the daughter, and from others, is a general endorsement of the first dress as perfect for her because she herself is perfect and two perfections compliment each other.

What we have done through transcendence is transform the conflict, making it more manageable. The word 'solution' is too absolute, as in solving clearly defined mathematical problems. Real life is more complicated. But through transformation in the direction of the blue dress the conflict somehow dissolves, like dew in the morning sun. And the mother seizes the transformation because she would like to get out of the corner she has painted herself into by putting her daughter under pressure. A modern accessory would solve the problem of the blue dress being old-fashioned. Happily she sets off for the reunion, in the right frame of mind for the 25th anniversary. Or so we hope.

The daughter then calls her boyfriend to say: 'The coast is clear.'

And did mother and daughter live happily ever after? Well yes, until the next conflict presented itself. And then the question arises whether they have learnt anything. Perhaps they could singly or together return to the original conflict. Perhaps the mother could reflect on why she did not choose the blue dress straight away, and why she had to put her daughter under such pressure. And the daughter might ask herself why she did not find the answer more quickly. Only when this happens has the conflict been 'processed' and the transcendence accepted so unconditionally that we can talk about a sustainable outcome. Any transformation is provisional only. The original conflict is still there until it evaporates, exposed to the heat of good processing.

Another example, guaranteed with no dress: a mobile phone. Rather inconsiderate, boorish, objectionable is he or she who has their phone switched on during a good dinner, a meeting, a lecture, a play, a concert, an opera – for instance in the midst of *Aida* in, say, Tbilisi. 'I am expecting an important message' – fine, good, stay at home or wait outside for the message.

The question is how to say that to 25–30 eager participants in a working group. Here are some norms and rules:

- You shall protect the group and yourself against such interruptions!
- You shall not be too accusatory and moralising!

In other words, you shall say it without saying it. A message in writing, or body language by showing your own telephone and how to switch it off, with a smile is still somewhat judgemental.

My friend, the superb Norwegian peace researcher Jörgen Johansen, has come up with a good solution: 'Remember to switch on your phones again after the seminar so that you don't miss any important messages!' Excellent. Constructive and future-oriented at the same time, as the phone has to be switched off in order for us to be able to switch it on again.

The message is received with a smile, and click, click, click.

Again the same question: how do we learn things like that?

Life is a school, good; but in that case there are many who have not yet enrolled in kindergarten. My own experience is that no nation is so socially adept as the North Americans, possibly because their pluralistic society forces them to find formulas that are conflict dissolving, or at least not conflict producing. In saying so we are not saying that all North Americans are equally competent. And between the genders women are better, not only 'more considerate', but socially 'more capable'. Don't men understand such things unless it's shouted at them, or written up in big letters in front of them?

Transcendence, in short, is the art of finding a both/and formula. In doing so the conflict is transformed because we have modified and twisted the goals a little. If this transformation is accepted and in addition is sustainable, then we can talk about a 'solution'. An expensive dress far beyond the means of the mother, and for that reason not sustainable, would not have been a solution. We have also come some distance if all parties find the transformed conflict is easier to live with. But things may also get worse: the transformation may bring us from the ashes to the fire: 'The blue dress was the dress my mother was wearing on the day she died.' In that case we can talk not about transformation but 'wrongformation' of the conflict. The conflict has reached deadlock. Creativity is good, but deep empathy is also needed.

Finally: don't start seeing contradiction = conflict everywhere:

The student: I so much want to have a richer inner life! I want to meditate, to *read* the mystics, to *live* the mystics. But I also love my skateboard and the Porsche. They're difficult to live without.

In Norway there used to be a saying, he who has 'given himself to the world' and he who has 'given himself to God', and a conflict between those two lifestyles. But not in California. There you can meditate on a skateboard or in a Porsche. Material things are trivialities for many and for that reason not necessarily in contradiction with the spiritual. The lifestyles mesh. It all depends on where, when and how it is done.

THE SUN

Once upon a time there were two neighbours, A and B. They lived in pretty houses with pretty gardens, and the whole thing looked as in the diagram.

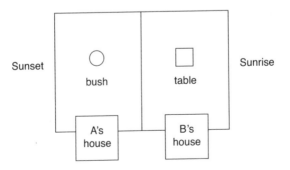

A and B are both fundamentalists, but of different kinds.

A is a *garden fundamentalist* and has just planted a small bush in front of his house. He enjoys watching it grow, like a little cub gradually filling the coat of skin it has been allocated. B is a *coffee fundamentalist*, and for him the high point of the day is coffee at sunset, which reminds him of the good old days when his house was the only one there, without neighbours.

The reader already senses the tragedy coming. The bush is growing out of control, high, wide, in all directions, including in depth in order to suck up more nutrition for all this growth – and above all in density. A is enjoying the complete realisation of his goal, the fully mature bush. At the same time B sees his goal – coffee at sunset, not just coffee – being reduced to a shadow of its former self.

Conflict Worker: please, go ahead and find a conflict transformation which has a solution for both parties, in other words, something that is acceptable and sustainable in the whole A–B system. There is of course a traditional (US?) outcome: B buys a chain saw with a silencer and during the night cuts down the full-grown bush at its base and then extracts the root, whereupon A fetches a gun from his bedside table – perhaps intended for his wife and/or for himself – and kills B. Sustainable, but short of the mutually acceptable.

We sense immediately the inadequacy of the compromise. The bush is pruned, cut back and filters a pale sun to B, at the same time as A, joylessly, looks at his clipped bush. As mentioned, one of the theses of this book is that (almost) all compromises have this unreleased character even if compromise once in a while is the only outcome acceptable to all parties.

At this point the participants often split into two groups. There are those who have understood the point and think it is a question of jumping straight to the transcendence, guided by intuition, and that the outcome depends on a touch of genius. Sometimes, yes. But the other group has understood the point better. They start drawing the basic diagram with the two axes and the five points and each point shouting: Who am I, concretely? What do I mean in this conflict? That basic diagram is the carrier of a systematic method, what philosophers call a heuristic and mathematicians an algorithm. Let us only hasten to add that it comes with no guarantee that the figure will always produce an outcome that can be accepted. However, if such a thing exists, it can usually be classified by means of the five points. It is like the old Chinese proverb about how to help human beings in distress: I can give you a fish. But even better is to teach you how to fish. Well put, but that assumes that there are fish in the lake or river in the first place.

Start by identifying the extreme points in the diagram, the points at which each fundamentalist gets what he is asking for and the other nothing. A's happiness and B's unhappiness are easily described, the same applies the other way round. But B's happiness will be short-lived because the growth of a bush is 'natural' and for that reason in the eyes of A something that should be accepted. Cutting down the bush, however, is a crime against nature in addition to being a crime against another man's property, and for that reason unacceptable. Extremists often portray themselves as 'natural'.

That little neither/nor point down to the left is important. It may be indicative of a solution, or several. Thus, a neighbour, C, may talk nicely with both of them and make them give up their goals in favour of bible study in C's house. Or, he can accept both bush and coffee but invite them to enjoy both in his considerably larger garden. Or, together with neighbours D and E he may occupy both gardens, remove the bush and the coffee table in accordance with the United Nation's Charter Chapter 7 about peace enforcement, not peace-keeping. Whereupon A and B obediently give up bush and coffee as their respective goals.

All three are transcending in so far as they create a new reality. But they are also negative by negating, cancelling the original goals, even if it works out positively for the parties.

What remains is [5]: both/and, with a twist. There are several. B could change his taste in favour of the morning light, turning his back to the monster bush, enjoying coffee at sunrise instead of coffee at sunset. That solution is important, shaking us out of the traditional assumption that 'both parties have to yield, give something up in order for the solution to work'. Symmetry is not a goal in itself, and is actually a part of the poor man's conflict philosophy. Our goal is not burden equality, but finding something both parties can accept, and so sustainable that it becomes compelling, self-evident. This attitude to acceptability and sustainability is located in the parties, not in an outside mediator filled with assumptions about symmetry. In general symmetry is a good guide and asymmetry a poor point of departure. But not in this case.

Most people see another solution: the coffee table is used as a bridge across the border between the plots, north-east of the bush. A and B meet for morning coffee and for evening coffee. A sits on the north side so that he can enjoy his full-grown bush; B on the south side, still somewhat allergic to bushes. There is no shadow for the sun. Both/and: bush *and* sun coffee. And in addition they benefit from good neighbourliness, perhaps friendship.

And do they live happily ever after? Well. It may be that B doesn't like to get up early enough for coffee at sunrise, that A does not drink coffee at all, and that neither of them wants to drink coffee with the other. The solution brings some change, whether they reach it alone or via a conflict worker. Some 'new reality', maybe even too much. What else do we have?

C may enter the scene again, with his own ideas. But they are hardly sustainable even if they are accepted: C has to sacrifice much of his time and much of his garden. There is also the possibility that the parties will give up their goals rather than handing the conflict over to C. A may give up his bush, extracting the root; B may give up his coffee and remove the table. Both are unhappy but may derive some comfort from the circumstance that this neither/nor is symmetrical. They are more or less equally unhappy. There's some kind of negative transcendence.

At this point the conflict worker comes on the scene again to stimulate a deeper dialogue. A dialogue is always questioning, searching. But at the same time there is direction. The focus is no longer on *diagnosis*, mapping the conflict – we assume that by now they know the basic diagram quite well. Nor are we searching for *therapy*, solutions, outcomes that can be accepted – they are already on the table. We are now exploring *prognosis*, predictions. If A really is going to stick to his full-grown bush, it is not unreasonable for the conflict worker to ask:

'A, how do you think B is going to react in the longer run?'
'He has to acquiesce!'
'Would you have done so in his place?'
'Of course not! But I am a real man, he is not!!'
'Do you think good neighbourly relations can result from all this?'
'Perhaps not, but that is beside the point. It's my garden, my bush!'
'In other words, one year will succeed the next without a neighbour to help you in the event of an emergency?'
'Hmm. You have a point there. Like a fire, for instance?'

The turning point in the dialogue usually comes when the other party's response changes from an exclamation mark to a question mark. A seems to be somewhat egoistic as a type, and that question hits home all right.

It is unnecessary to point out that a conflict worker has to have the map, the basic diagram for his inner eye, and at any time be able to plot all the outcomes in order to play out the comparisons. This often leads to results, and the more good solutions come up the better, as here.

It is considerably more difficult if the conflict is only apparently about the bush and coffee. To appreciate this we don't have to delve into the deeper recesses of A's and B's souls, or conflicts with others, X, Y and Z, that they are projecting onto the situation. There is another conflict that very often serves as a backdrop for the conflict that is being acted out, and that conflict is not about the bush and coffee, regardless of how important they may be. It is a conflict about *being right*, having justice *on one's side*. No longer are such concrete goals as the bush and coffee the focus, but rather the justification, the legitimisation of these goals. For instance:

A: This is my plot, it's my choice, and the bush is on my side!
B: It is on your side, but the shadow is on my plot and is causing me harm!

What justification will be supported by the legal process? To get the answer we go to court to see what the lawyers and judge can come up with. A court case is exactly about being found right, innocent, not liable – as opposed to wrong, guilty, liable. That's important.

But a court process is no good for transcendence and transformation. Both parties cannot be found right at the same time, nor can they be found partly right. Transcendence and compromise are both problematic in legal cases. We are essentially left with three possibilities: the classic 'A is right and B not', 'B is right and A not', and withdrawal expressed as 'The case is dismissed' and/or 'The parties are requested to find a solution themselves.' In other words: 'A won', 'B won', as in a duel, a tournament, a war, or Undecided/they withdrew'. The courts have a limited conflict outcome repertoire; only three out of five. Law is about legality, not about solutions.

What happens to the loser? He can appeal. But when that possibility has been exhausted, what next? In theory, the court system is in itself legitimate enough to legitimise a decision about legitimacy. But it is not easy to be the neighbour of someone who has won a court case against oneself and is enjoying 'I was right' to the full. Is this 'sustainable'? Acceptability is necessary in order to make a court decision sustainable, and stands in the way of revenge and revanche from the losing party. But an outcome also defines social relations between the parties. And bad social relations can in turn lead to low acceptability and low sustainability.

Sustainability in social relations is by and large incompatible with conflict processes that define winners and losers, and with a court case in particular. This argument is weakened if the parties do not intend to meet each other after the court case, as in separation or divorce proceedings. Their meetings will often be of short duration, violent, destructive. In short, there are good arguments for avoiding court cases among neighbours. It's better to go in for transcendence/ transformation.

Take a case about inheritance. If it is a question of a simple distribution among siblings according to a formula they in the end have accepted, then it is not so problematic. But if all of them insist on 'getting most' because the parents 'loved them most', then it is difficult to transcend the contradiction. 'Most to X' logically must exclude 'most to Y'.

Well – are we sure about that? Perhaps what is to be inherited can be divided in two, the immobile and the mobile, including money. They may take what is closest to their heart. Goals can be divided into sub-goals. With a little differentiation even logically watertight contradictions loosen up.

A boy: 'I like grandfather (90) and his stories better than father (50).' 'But what about fishing?' 'Well, father is better for that!' 'So perhaps half of the summer can be spent with father and half with grandfather?' A flat, symmetrical compromise. But next year all three go on holiday together. Father fishes, Grandfather tells stories and the boy enjoys the company of both. And they all enjoy each other's company.

There are many variations of the sun theme. Let us take a rain variation first. The map is still valid, but the plots are now located on a slope, and A's plot is higher up. There is a lot of rain in the district, but the gardens absorb the rain and send it down to the groundwater. One day, however, A covers parts of his plot with asphalt or flagstones – it is more beautiful that way he says. The bushes are converted into pot plants, well watered by the rain. But the rain water is no longer absorbed, flows down to B and his garden becomes waterlogged. In his basement there is suddenly a foot of water.

Here there is a possibility that is also available in the conflict over the bush and coffee: A and B literally withdraw. They sense years of quarrel ahead, move out, sell their houses to the highest bidder on a day the sun is shining brightly. Roughly speaking, everything said above is also valid for this conflict. But transcendence has to be very concrete. Thus, they could have a joint water reservoir. A system of ditches and pipes diverting the water from A past B's plot would eliminate the damage to B. But it is less creative and cooperative than a joint water reservoir.

Let us take another variation bringing in a view. A is now located lower than B and closer to the ocean, the beach. The sun that sets in the west is not just any sun, but the sun saying goodnight in the Norwegian sea, off the western coast. B and his parents, and his grandparents before that, have enjoyed the view until the day it became clear that A was planning to erect a garage between B and the sunset. There is nowhere else to site the garage, the plot is simply too small.

One possible solution is easily seen by some, more difficult or never by others: to sink the garage half way down. The two neighbours could find a formula for sharing the costs. And they would of course have a giant party to celebrate the garage by the sea and live happily ever after. Until one of the wives has a 25th anniversary.

THE WARDROBE

Johan (peace researcher, conflict worker): We have a house in Spain, friends often visit us, usually a couple, he and she, and usually with a PC. In postmodern life there is much searching for sockets and telephone plugs in order to overcome geographical distance. When we decided to build a cottage in the garden for our visitors, with a bed, a table and modems for two – and in addition a kitchen bench, shower/WC and all of that on a very small plot – the furnishing was more or less fixed in advance.

Fumiko (Johan's Japanese wife, peace researcher and conflict worker): The idea was good. But when I saw the drawing something was clearly missing and I asked immediately: where's the wardrobe? It was clear from Johan's voice and his flickering eyes that he had overlooked it, but as a man didn't want to admit it. His answer was odd:

Johan:	Wardrobe? This is Spain, they hardly need any clothes at all except swimming trunks and a swimsuit – the swimming pool is right outside the cottage!
Fumiko:	Silence. The look.
Johan:	OK, perhaps they need some clothes. But they can put them in a suitcase or two, and then the suitcases can go under the bed!
Fumiko:	Silence. The look.
Johan:	OK. They need a wardrobe. But there isn't enough floor space! And I cannot get rid of one of the tables because then all our feminist friends will say that they know who we think is not going to use a PC! Catastrophe. But we have a wardrobe in the garage. They can leave the cottage, go down the steps into the garage and put their clothes there!
Fumiko:	Typical of men in general. Of Johan in particular! And – the look again.

The mood was sombre. We went to bed, but have an agreement that quarrels are not carried over to the next morning.

The problem was that sleeping did not help, usually a good formula for a both/and to emerge. Fumiko was dreaming of guests walking restlessly around with unopened suitcases; Johan was dreaming about a monster wardrobe breaking into the cottage, eating one table, then wallowing on the floor.

Next morning the carpenter, Jose – Pepe to Spaniards – arrived from the neighbouring village. He was supposed to be fixing something for the kitchen bench. Johan said, 'Pepe, we have a problem' and described the conflict about too little space for both the PC tables and the wardrobe, without necessarily personalising the conflict in terms of the advocates. After two seconds:

| *Pepe*: | Problem? I don't see any problem at all. All you need to do is just – |
| *Conflict Worker*: | Yes, what did Pepe say? |

The extreme positions are clear: Johan gets his way, no wardrobe at all (adding the suitcase or the garage 'solutions'); Fumiko gets her way, a wardrobe, she will decide where, and the tables disappear, both of them. It is also quite clear what the compromise would be: one very small wardrobe, two very small tables. Big enough for the

PCs, but not for papers and books. And the wardrobe would be too small to accommodate enough hangers. Everybody would be left unsatisfied. Where is the transcending solution?

Some people see the solution immediately, others not. It is obvious once formulated, and carries with it a new architectonic reality:

Pepe: Use the walls. Put the cupboards close to the ceiling for shirts and blouses, for socks and underwear; with some iron rods to hang the hangers on for dresses and jackets and things of that kind.

Conclusion: Johan and Fumiko had a more social than architectonic imagination, whereas Pepe could draw on his professionalism and experience with houses, their owners and their wardrobes.

The conflict worker couple evidently had some kind of obsession with floors, with two-dimensional rather than three-dimensional space, probably a subconscious fixation. Very embarrassing for Johan given his mathematical background. And even more so because he is so fond of telling two stories, one about a man at the South Pole, the other about a poor mouse.

Once upon a time there was a man at the South Pole who heard a deep voice from heaven: 'You shall move ten centimetres, but you are not permitted to go to the north. If you are not able to do this, you will be frozen into ice!'

Every step ahead is a step to the north. The alternative to becoming an ice statue is, however, obvious once it has been pointed out: jump ten centimetres.

Once upon a time there was a small mouse whom a sadistic psychologist had placed in a maze in order to measure 'behaviour under cross-pressure'. In front of all exits highly tempting morsels of cheese and meat had been placed. But in between there was acid, electric shocks, fire and other disincentives. Fortunately, the mouse had a mobile phone and called a conflict worker to get some advice about how the positive goals could be obtained and the negative goals avoided. The conflict worker asked immediately whether there was a ceiling to the maze. There was none. 'Start running', he said, 'run as fast as you can, then jump!' And the mouse emerged unscathed, right in front of the delicacies.

All three are examples of an important source of creativity: identifying *the forgotten dimension*, or variable. In all three cases the dimension was trivial and geometrical: height, upward. All three illustrate how we are tied to the two-dimensional floor, glacier, surface of the earth. If Einstein used four-dimensional space to formulate his theory of relativity – transcending classical Newtonian physics tied to three-dimensional Euclidean space – then the rest of us should at least be able to look upward and contemplate three-dimensional space.

Two sources of creativity have been mentioned so far. First, bring in from experience a conflict with a known solution according to the 'that reminds me of' principle, and then translate from one conflict to the other. Second, ask the question, could there be some assumptions the parties to the conflict have in common, and is that consensus blocking creativity? Such assumptions are usually quite evident, trivial even, not worth formulating. They are subconscious. In other words, the conflict worker has to learn to hear what has not been said and to see the invisible. To identify the assumptions and twist them, gently.

INFIDELITY

We proceed from the wardrobe to infidelity, both possible components of a marriage.

The Woman: It had been going on for some years, and with my best friend! I was the only one who didn't know. One day he had forgotten to erase a message on the answerphone about where and when. A woman's voice which I recognised. I went to the rendezvous, hiding behind a tree and got my worst suspicions confirmed. I was so angry I could have killed them both, but had no gun. And now everything has collapsed, everything – and we had such wonderful children, good parents, friends, neighbours, colleagues, a perfect house –

The Man: I have the best wife in the world, but what was going to happen happened. It was not in her best interests, my wife, that is clear enough; but what I did was not against her either. It just happened that way. It is psychologically completely possible to be in love with two women, and physically completely possible to make love to two women. But socially it is impossible. I know that, I understand it. And now everything has fallen apart, everything. And we have such a fine house, wonderful children, good parents, friends, neighbours, colleagues – I have lost everything, two wonderful women, just because of a stupid answerphone!

The Other Woman: He has betrayed his wife and I have betrayed my best friend. I do not know which is worse. I feel such a creep, so small. And I have felt like that for a long time, but I was unable to say no. He was so tender, so good to me, and said something about her possibly also having someone on the side. I found comfort in that. He never compared us, but said that he was fond of us both. I also found comfort in that. And she and I were best friends in kindergarten, we shared everything, so I was thinking perhaps it would work out. And now everything has collapsed, their marriage, our friendship. I am the lowest of the low. What I would really like to do is simply vanish. But I am too much of a coward!

This is the first case where violence has come into the picture, with clear thoughts about homicide and suicide among people who are suffering, and who have directly or indirectly harmed and hurt each other. The other examples are more like puzzles, easy or complicated, but not very emotional. These three are simply in need of help, particularly the woman and the man, who see their marriage falling apart.

The question is how. It has sometimes been my task as a conflict worker also to work on such conflicts. Some experience has accumulated and can be shared with others.

In workshops a number of answers emerge, from immediate divorce to immediate reconciliation, with apologies and forgiveness. But as usual we have to try to be systematic. No conflict is sacred. No conflict can escape that little diagram. All we have to do is clarify the goals of the parties, and at that point the three statements above may be obscuring the issues rather than clarifying them. All three are portraying themselves a little bit too simplistically.

Perhaps the woman could imagine a man making a pass at her, including her husband's best friend? And maybe in that case the moral calculus would be more balanced if the husband went ahead into infidelity so that she could seek cover behind that?

Possibly, the husband was jealous of the best friend because she had so much of his wife's confidence.

And, possibly, even if that woman was the best friend they might have been in a competitive relationship from childhood. Her girlfriend had got the best boy in town, the most attractive, the one with the best career, the biggest house, the most powerful car. She was unmarried. In her self-declaration as the lowest of the low there might also have been a sting of triumph.

In short, the goals are not that simple when looked at in more depth. But if we include all of this, aren't we heading for psychoanalysis for all three?

Yes, if we believe that the road to peace passes through the process of uncovering the past. But in the TRANSCEND method the road ahead should instead pass through images of a constructive future.

Let us start once again with a major rule in conflict work: take as the point of departure the self-presentation by the parties and their own analysis. Let us use a clear example: if a party refers to itself as a 'liberation front' then the conflict worker shall not refer to them as 'terrorists'. Here we go:

The Woman:	A marriage is only genuine if it is based on fidelity.
The Man:	A marriage can benefit from renewal through infidelity.
The Other Woman:	I only wish I had been able to say no.

Let us use this as a point of departure, even if the woman may be somewhat too ideological, the man too innovative in his attempt to avoid any blame ('I did it for our sake, to breathe more life into our relationship') and the other woman simply dishonest. Sexual hunger is a strong drive, perhaps even stronger than conventional hunger. Female sexuality may be more comprehensive, perhaps less one-sidedly genital. But all of that enforces rather than weakens the dishonesty thesis.

Let's exclude the other woman to get started and concentrate on the marital partners. Fidelity excludes infidelity, the goal of the woman excludes the goal of the man, so we have a clear contradiction. Can it be transcended? There is a well-known compromise: the man limits his infidelity to X weeks a year, and the woman her fidelity to 52

– X weeks, or something in that direction. The woman becomes somewhat less absolutist, while the man is now operating under a self-imposed constraint. They can have additional rules like 'Not with anybody I know', 'I don't want to know who it is', 'Never reveal any details', 'The first priority is always each other.'

An objection might be that the woman is yielding more than the man. The opposite would be the case if the man enters his marriage fully and turns the pleasures he is renouncing into self-development and love for his wife.

But this is not transcendence, for that the contradiction between fidelity and infidelity is too massive, too logical. We could of course twist the concepts a little, like introducing fidelity in a triangle, let the other woman enter the relationship and convert infidelity in the marriage into fidelity within a *ménage à trois*. But imagine that all three of them, or two or even only one of them cannot accept that formula, then what?

Let us try the general rule for logical conflicts and differentiate. So far we have followed the usual language in our one-sided culture and interpreted infidelity sexually: the infidelity of the body – or a little part of the body. Let us get out of that frame. How about the infidelity of the mind, of the spirit, how about economic and social infidelity?

What will the conflict worker have to do to expand the frame of reference? A very stupid approach is to summon the marriage partners to his office, adopt a serious yet compassionate demeanour and pronounce with a voice filled with deep sorrow 'tell me what actually happened'.

First, this will play off one against the other and set the scene for a verbal duel in which they are probably already consciously and subconsciously very well practised.

Second, they may become dishonest because they now have an attentive audience, the conflict worker. As women often talk more, more fluently and more convincingly about emotional matters than men, the man can use a simple strategy: let her talk, as much as possible, and then signal with his eyes to the conflict worker 'Now can you see my problem?' The woman can have a corresponding strategy, 'You first', and trust that the man will be as silent, primitive, dishonest and as transparent as he usually is. And then signal with her eyes, 'Now can you see my problem?'

But most importantly, third: by focusing negatively on the near past we end up very far from a positive, constructive future – as mentioned, a major point in the TRANSCEND method. Transcendence presupposes hope, and hope is located in visions of a positive, constructive future, not in rehashing a traumatic past.

What the conflict worker has to do is launch deep dialogues, not debates, with the marital partners, but with one at a time. Grammatically he/she should talk 'future, constructive', not 'past, destructive':

'What's your idea of a good marriage?'
'That's impossible with him, the way he carries on!'
'Could you imagine putting that aside for a while; we will return to that later. Now, how do you imagine a good marriage?'
'There has to be fidelity, he cannot have others!'
'And the woman?'
'That applies to her as well, of course!'
'Do you mean that if there is sexual fidelity on both sides everything will work out?'
'No, but it's a precondition. There also has to be love.'
'What do you mean by that?'
'Warmth in the soul, not only in the body.'
'Beautiful. Sharing feelings, memories, expectations, isn't that it?'
'Precisely. And the union of the bodies to confirm it.'
'But how about a common goal? Something that you really can do together?'
'That's obvious, home making, bringing children into the world!'
'But the home can become a routine. And the children will sooner or later leave the nest. Then what?'
'Yes, no – I haven't really thought through that. And that is exactly the position we're in, we are in our mid-forties –'
'What kind of projects do you have now?'
'Well, my husband has his career, and the business is going well. I have become interested in religion, in Buddhism.'
'Something in common?'
'No, we are walking separately, on different roads – is that something you are getting at, are you indicating that that was the reason why he was unfaithful?'
'Let's continue for a while talking in general, not only about the two of you.'

Many will nod in recognition at much of this. Love is the union of the body and the union of the soul of two human beings. But there is also the spirit, capable of reflecting on body and soul and setting new goals, 'reprogramming' (reinventing) itself. The problem is not necessarily that the wrong programme is driving them apart. It may be that they have no programme at all. *A joint life project*, after the children have left the nest, but before the joint project of keeping each other alive as long as possible.

Of course, both of them can have their individual projects, as well as with others. But if that takes the place of a joint marital project – culturally, religiously, politically, economically, socially – then we may be close to spiritual infidelity. The marital partner should be the first choice as a partner for the union of the spirits. If not, what they are seeking in their adventures may be something far beyond the union of bodies and the closeness of the souls, or a joint project. The beginning may be 'infidelity' as a project. 'It's only about sex' becomes a statement that should be regarded with considerable scepticism. They are looking for more.

'Do you love your husband in spite of all this?'
'Yes, and that is what hurts! But he doesn't love me.'
'How do you know that?'
'He was unfaithful. Could he have been if he really loved me?!'
'Are you sure? Maybe you did not have enough in common for a fulfilling life together? And how about financial matters? The social aspects? Are you running the home like a joint enterprise, fully transparently? No secret accounts? Are you supporting each other socially when you are with friends and colleagues?'
'I get my "housekeeping money" from him; that's enough to save a little and have my private account, only for me. And I support him in everything, even if his business is of no interest me. And all he does is make fun of my Buddhism!'

Enough. Evidently they have many other problems. And after this there is a corresponding dialogue with the husband, not only to get his view of sexual infidelity, but also to get his marital philosophy and how he views their relationship when the focus is on more aspects of marriage.

From the sexual we have now advanced to five types of fidelity and infidelity (the body, the soul, the spirit, money matters and social aspects). With two partners we get ten goals. In doing so we have obtained three things:

(1) We have relativised sexual infidelity, put it in a context so that it doesn't dominate the field.

(2) We have arrived at a model for a good marriage, more fidelity than infidelity; and

(3) We have arrived at a model for a bad marriage: more infidelity than fidelity, from +10 to –10. And we have a basis for concrete advice:

- Don't take infidelity too seriously. If everything else is OK, don't let it destroy something good, organic. You feel that warmth for each other, you have a joint life project, you are running the household like a business with full transparency, and you are supporting each other in all kinds of occasions.

- Monogamy, if practised only sexually, is not sufficient. You are clinging to it precisely because everything else has gone wrong. Either you have to start working deeply on the other four dimensions or my advice would be that you separate before something really goes wrong, in spite of sexual fidelity. That has become a joint project you are proud of – but it is also part of something that is cold and mutually controlling, which is dominating your relationship, supported by religious formulas neither of you really believe in.

Harsh words? Perhaps they have to be adjusted to the party to the dialogue. But there is something worse than harsh words. Two lives wasted in a prison where both are simultaneously prisoner and guard.

What about the other woman? Everything conspires to make hers a forgotten role. The focus has been on the marital partners. They are the ones who are seeking help and assistance from friends, counsellors, the courts – in the final analysis to be shown to be in the right. The other woman sees that it is in her interest to keep a low profile. In parts of patriarchal culture she would be seen as the snake in the grass 'who tempted that poor man beyond endurance'.

But she won't be forgotten if the conflict worker does his/her job. To have a dialogue with *all* parties in a conflict is the duty of the conflict worker, to map their goals, to stimulate the creativity of the parties, to play creative proposals back to them. Possibly her relationship to the man, everything considered, is more promising than the marital relationship. But let us assume that that is not the case. If the conflict worker has participated in saving a marriage, how about saving a friendship? Could this not also be a strong tie, along three of the dimensions, one worthy of being preserved?

But how? By exploring, very carefully, whether the three people at some point or another may have a future vision where they could put all of this behind them, mobilise a little humour and build both marriage and friendship. Perhaps even build it together, in a triangle enriched with a deep, if traumatic, experience. Not easy, but very enriching.

A friendship is something simpler than a marriage. But we can still talk about three of the five, the fidelity of the soul, the spirit, and social fidelity. To share sorrow and joy, to have a project even one not that deep, to support each other socially – all that and more would form part of a friendship. And the road ahead is not called 'time heals all wounds'. If the wounds have become less visible this may be because they are now located deeper in the soul. And that's where the repair work has to take place. A joint life project is indispensable. We explore the future to be better able to return to the past. The road ahead also has to pass through reconciliation, truth and forgiveness. The truth about all of them, and forgiveness from all of them. But how?

Let us first look at the concepts. To forgive does not mean to forget; deep wounds cannot be forgotten. But there are some excellent formulations: 'Let us put it behind us', 'That's over now, let's move on', 'A new chapter/book in our relationship.' This can be understood as a contract not to repeat past errors, not to bring up the past unless it is repeated.

'Sorry' one of them says. And he or she may add 'Can you accept my apology?' 'Yes, I can.' Simple words, yes, but sometimes very difficult to say. 'Can you forgive me?' goes even deeper and is even more future-oriented. In a Christian culture it reminds people of the Lord's Prayer: 'Forgive us our trespasses as we forgive those who trespass against us.' This is a prayer about reconciliation in a triangle: 'If I forgive, dear Lord, will you reward me by forgiving me?' and/or 'Because you forgive us then we should also be forgiving.' If that helps, good. But apologies, forgiveness, some kind of compensation, even if reduced to a bouquet of flowers, do not presuppose faith in a god who does the bookkeeping for everybody and everything. To the contrary, the religious dimension can also stand in the way of direct forgiveness and reconciliation because 'only God can forgive'. As a result we get many human beings who build their lives around a trauma that once afflicted them and offended them rather than bringing it out in the open; ask for and get an apology and forgiveness, adding some ritual of reconciliation from a handshake with eye contact and a warm embrace to a good party or better. Both sides can then stand tall, relieved of the burden.

For this to take place some truth must be put on the table. But the whole truth can make matters worse. What is implicit is often better left unsaid. Harm hurts even more if it comes from a wicked intention, so it may be better not to be too explicit. And some gently applied humour may be helpful.

We are left with a number of possible solutions, as well as a number of possible approaches or methods. Things may be complicated by bringing in children, parents (-in-law), friends, neighbours, colleagues. How much do they mean to the couple and the couple to them? An indifferent environment can be an argument for separation if the ties that once held the couple together have become threadbare, or are absent. A social environment with a lively and healthy interest in maintaining the relationship should be taken seriously, as joint 'social capital'.

Here we are touching on an important theoretical, and for that reason practical, point; nothing is as practical as a good theory. The word 'complicate' has been used. In the theory of conflict this is a positive word. The most troubling conflicts are the logical ones between two parties, like two spouses with fidelity/infidelity as goals. Everything becomes so naked, there is no flexibility in any direction, nothing that can be negotiated or traded or anything else. All mental activity, all emotions are directed towards that dramatic contradiction, and the parties experience themselves like Adam and Eve, alone in the world.

Introduce more goals, possibly by differentiating the goals that are there; introduce more parties to whom the outcome of the conflict is important enough to become a goal, and then we may get closer to transcendence and transformation.

As a measure of *complexity* we can use the sum of the number of parties and the number of goals. That is the kind of thing we have to have in mind when we are mapping the conflict, or the sum of all goals for all parties, for that is what we need when we arrive at how many goals there are. The more complexity, the more possibilities for contradictions. But the more contradictions the more possibilities to trade off against the other ('OK, I'll promise to be faithful if you can become more interested in my business'). But this is where we stop.

This book is mainly about *elementary* conflicts, with two goals. The theory for *complex* conflicts is exactly that, more complex.

SIESTA AND FIESTA

He is Japanese, she is Filipina; they are newly married and live in Tokyo. The marriage works very well on Monday, Tuesday, Wednesday, Thursday, Friday and Saturday. Sunday is a catastrophe.

He is of the opinion that he has worked hard all week and could use some relaxation, on a couch, in front of the TV, as a 'couch potato' with some finger food in front of him. In short, a *siesta*.

She is of the opinion that she has worked hard all week and could use some relaxation. Her idea of relaxation is a party with ten to twenty friends, lasting from 10 am to 4 pm, with drinks and warm food, music and dancing, fun. In short, *fiesta*.

Another Sunday is approaching. Both of them think with horror about what they know is going to happen, namely nothing, only an unsolved problem looming like a dark shadow between them, a monster in the corner of the living room.

Husband:	This is how we do things in Japan, and that is where we are living. In addition to that, I hate to say it, but here the man makes the decisions!
She:	This is the way we do things in the Philippines. I am a good Japanese six days a week, and that should be enough. The days of patriarchy are over, I have the right to decide on at least one day!
Conflict Worker:	Well, what are we doing now?

The *extreme positions* are clear:

His Sunday:	Silence in front of the TV, eyes flickering, the TV flickering, and slowly he sinks back into the couch, catches up with some sleep after long train journeys, working days, visits to the bars.
Her Sunday:	Life and laughter, colour and sound, happy human beings.

He withdraws to the bedroom before the guests arrive.

The *compromise* is as usual unsatisfactory for both: half a Sunday devoted to each activity, or alternate Sundays, his or hers. The same applies to *negative transcendence*, a walk in the park every Sunday.

But then we come to *positive transcendence*. I had the advantage as conflict worker that I had been through a 'this reminds me of'. In Honolulu, Hawai'i, we have some friends, a couple, he is a professor of English and the theory of biography, she a lawyer for the economically less privileged.

He loves American football with the teams dressed up in helmets and other types of protective gear, and wants a party round the TV once a year, on the Sunday of the Superbowl, the finals. He invites his professorial friends; all of them are getting on in years. They are sitting with whisky glasses in hand, urging on their heroes, 'Get him!' 'Right on, now!'

She, like me, hates American football, machismo, violence and invites her friends to a party the same day, in the same room. In the middle of the room is the TV and the game is watched from the couch as the party unfolds on the margins of the room, with delicious small dishes, fragrances and colour as in Hawai'i, drinks considerably more varied than whisky, and a buffet. What now happens is just as one would expect: slowly there is some exchange between the He section and the She section of the party. Some of them are drifting towards the TV in order to get their prejudices confirmed. Others are drifting towards the aromas and colours. By and large the groups stick to the Superbowl or party. But they are also open to a rich both/and to the benefit of all.

So this became the proposal, with the variation that in Tokyo the TV is placed in the corner, and the couch is turned so that it has its back to the room. There was hardly enough space for the fiesta since it had to be shared with an element of siesta – without sleep, however. The exchange between the parties was frequent; he participated a little, she got some TV news and the weather forecast.

The whole thing worked because the total proposal included negative transcendence [3] to a park the coming Sunday, compromise [4] with siesta the second Sunday and fiesta the third Sunday, and then positive transcendence [5] together in the same room the fourth Sunday. The whole main diagonal, *the peace diagonal* [3] + [4] + [5] became the transformation menu. In the end they landed on [5] and lived happily the whole week – including Sundays.

GUESS WHO'S COMING TO DINNER?

She, a brilliant Japanese Hawai'ian student, perfect in Japanese, came to my office and told me what had happened:

- My father was detained in a concentration camp after Pearl Harbor, like most Japanese Americans in the USA. Japanese Americans were seen as potential traitors, moreover they could be used as bargaining chips against American prisoners of war. After the war they were released. But 50 years had to pass before President Clinton apologised, and there was some compensation for those who were still alive.
- My father was very active in that struggle. His argument was that even if we had Japanese parentage, we were just as good Americans as anybody else, and the whole concentration camp was racist, simply based on the way we looked. In the end these arguments made some impact in Washington DC. Congress passed a law about compensation.
- Yesterday, catastrophe struck. I had asked whether my boyfriend could come for dinner and my parents had said yes, with pleasure. He is black, an African American, was in the military here in Hawai'i until he refused to go to Vietnam and became a student. My father opened the door. When he saw my boyfriend he shouted: 'Is he the one you are going out with! Get out both of you and never return!' Very much like what happened to Sidney Poitier in the movie *Guess Who's Coming to Dinner?*
- We disappeared. Father was distraught. My friend was surprised, but also embarrassed because he did not want to cause problems for me. I am very fond of him and am not going to give him up for anything in the world, not even for my father's love. Right now it looks as if I have to give up one of them, my father or my boyfriend. Can you see some way out of this – isn't that what you are lecturing about!?

Author: Well, dear reader, can you see some exit? In the dialogue neither/nor, to give up both the friend and the father, as some kind of protest, was at the bottom of the list. Compromise, to see both of them once in a while, not more, met with no acceptance. As the conflict has a rather absolute character, 'You have to choose between him and me', we have to start differentiating.

At this point protests are emerging:

- But the father's position is invalid, illegitimate! He is a racist, exactly what he accuses the government in Washington of being. He has to look into himself, acknowledge his own racism.

He is the one who has to apologise and help the young people starting out on life!

That reaction is understandable, but hardly a good point of departure for solving a conflict. To catch another person in a contradiction, between accusing others of racism and then practising it oneself, belongs to a culture of debate, not to a culture of dialogue. A debate is a fight with verbal, not physical weapons (in French *battre* = beat). The victory usually goes to he who can catch the other in more contradictions: 'Five minutes ago you said this, now you are saying exactly the opposite'; 'What you say is not in accordance with the latest report from the UN.' A dialogue, *dia logos*, through the word, by using words, is something quite different. There is no competition to win a battle of words. The parties are working together to find a solution to a problem. And the first move is not triumphantly to point out the contradiction, but possibly to ask what a good marriage for his wonderful daughter would look like. Constructive and future-oriented.

But sooner or later the dialogue also has to reflect on what happened yesterday. The past, however, is so much easier to process when the work on an acceptable future has been done. It is so much easier to work in a tunnel when there is a glimmer of light at the far end.

'What do you want for your daughter?' is a better point of departure than 'What do you have against that boyfriend?' And it very quickly became evident that he wants her personal happiness. But he also wishes that she, like he himself, would be a bearer of Japanese culture in US society, that her children would learn the Japanese language and would be culturally competent in both the Japanese and American cultures. The problem with the boyfriend is not his colour, nor is it 'mixed blood'. But the father assumed that a coloured person would be less understanding of and positive to a Japanese cultural project, and that the daughter would become 'only' American.

The rest became a question of convincing him that the opposite is true. A black American is also living in two cultures, the usual American culture and an African-American culture with a somewhat special English, with its own music and art, traumatic memories, myths. This is not a new problem. But the couple would have to be tri-cultural rather than bi-cultural – a rich combination, in other words. He would possibly also have as a condition that their children should be bearers of African-American culture as well as of Japanese culture, and with that be able to move comfortably in the highly diverse American social space.

But how to convey this to the father when contact with the daughter and her boyfriend had been broken and her professor was a Norwegian who was much younger than the father? The solution was a Japanese Zen priest, older than the father and deeply rooted in his culture. He gave the father the time he needed to arrive at the solution. In the Japanese patriarchal culture the road to his heart passed through neither his wife nor his daughter, but came from above, and passed from one man to the other.

The key to the transcendence was to understand that the core of the problem was not race, but culture. What the father wanted was grandchildren who could be bearers of Japanese culture, not necessarily of Japanese skin colour. And thus the conflict came to an end.

THE PARENTS, THE CHILDREN AND THE GOOD HOUSE

Dear Ann Landers,
What shall I do with my parents? They never leave me in peace. They are always nagging, 'Hang up your clothes', 'Tidy your room', 'Give others a chance to use the phone.' Nagging all the time, never any peace and quiet. Please help me, what shall I do?
  No peace.

Dear No Peace,
Hang up your clothes. Tidy up your room. Let others use the phone.
  Ann Landers

Good answers for the simple reason that parent goals like 'clothes on hangers, tidy rooms, and incoming and outgoing telephone calls for everybody' very often are legitimate goals. The goals of the children 'I want to do exactly what I want with *my* clothes, it's my room, I must talk with my friends' are not always at the same level of legitimacy. What kind of process legitimises the goals of the parents in the children is another matter. This is often referred to as 'raising the children'. A frightening expression. Like pulling them up. From what? To what? By the hair?

What happens in puberty is often that children to an ever-increasing extent experience the goals their parents have for them as illegitimate:

Daughter/son, 16 years old: They interfere with even the smallest things, how we dress, who we go out with, what time we come home at night, what time we go to bed, when we switch off the light. I can't stand this micro-control of everything possible. I am old enough to wash myself. OK, I am going to make a few mistakes. But they will be my mistakes and I can learn from them. I can't go on being a dependant of these inhabitants of the past. I am moving out, living alone. Auntie has a room she can let me have.

Father/Mother, early forties: The problem is that he/she is not yet really mature enough to know where the borderline is between the exciting, and the stupid, illegitimate and plainly illegal. She/he hates having to come home, go to bed and all that. But the consequences of letting them decide for themselves can be catastrophic, particularly for her/him. We cannot let her/him live with our sister even if they like each other – sooner or later problems will arise related to money, food, laundry –

Conflict Worker: It's a universal theme. What advice are we going to give them? Wait until the problem solves itself because they will move out in due course to study, for work? And the children are not totally honest. They demand independence, but they are also a bit frightened. And the parents are also dishonest. They are afraid of losing power, they are afraid they will miss their children and they are afraid of the loneliness that will come when there's just the two of them.

The children want to distance themselves in order to be able to cultivate their independence. And the parents want closeness both to control them and to give and get love 'just like when they were small'. Distance and closeness look very much like logically excluding each other.

One possible transcendence of this contradiction is purely technical-architectonic: a room within the parents' apartment with its own shower/WC, perhaps a kitchenette and fridge, a door to the rest of the house/apartment, but also their own front door. This is very common in the USA, together with many other superb layouts; but more rare in Japan and most European countries. Perhaps it costs a bit more, but very little relative to the costs of moving out, let alone the social costs of two generations living too closely together.

Declarations of independence from teenagers come at an ever younger age, two-generation apartments/houses will also become more common. The same will happen to three-generation solutions as the age of retirement falls and life expectancy increases. In the old days the solution in the countryside was a cottage built to one side; today that would be too land-intensive. The balance between control and mutual aid will move, but the principle that distance and closeness have to be reconciled will remain. Psychologists and others don't have to feel ashamed if they resort to architectonic/technical solutions. But they should feel ashamed if they know nothing about them.

The problem is the same for two and three nations within one state. Autonomy, self-rule, presupposes one's own territory (room). But these territories can be within the same country (apartment, house), with a relatively open border (but knock on the door first!) but with one's own exit to the outside world. National independence movements often like to have access to the ocean or to other countries. Enclosed 'enclaves' are not popular. If parents/countries are willing to give children/nations equal dignity, 'taking them seriously', listening to them, then their well-intended advice will be more readily accepted, as for instance by Samis and Tamils. And indeed Palestinians.

THE WOMAN, THE MAN AND THE GOOD LIFE

The Woman: My problem is easily formulated: I am greedy! I want everything. I want to continue my career as a university professor, to do research, to read, write books, attend conferences, seminars, to become an expert, get official commissions. And I would like to have a husband of whom I can be proud, one who loves me as much as I love him. I do not want financial worries. But believe me, I am not thinking only of myself, I would also like to work politically for others. I want a beautiful but also practical home which can be a centre for our friends, and beautiful, clever children. I can see in your eyes that you want to ask that question: yes, maybe a little adventure now and then!

I want to travel, see the world. I want to enjoy art, literature, music, exhibitions. And – not least in all of this – I want to become a richer person inside myself. I am still a child who has neglected the inner life, and I don't know what to do.

Go ahead, try to find a both/and solution for that one!

The Man: My problem is easily formulated: I am greedy! I want everything. I want to continue my career as a businessman. But the goal is not to be rich. Far from it. The goal is to beat others, to own the market in that branch even if it costs blood. I want a wife, home and children and all that, I am a little bit old-fashioned in that regard. I see in your eyes that you want to ask that question: yes, perhaps an adventure now and then!

I want to travel, see the world. I want to enjoy art, literature, music, exhibitions. And – not least in all of this – I want to be a richer person inside myself, I am still a little child who has neglected his inner life, I do not know how.

Go ahead, try to find a both/and solution for this one!

Conflict Worker: These aren't so unusual. In both the goals are lining up.

As usual we have to start with a conflict analysis and bring the problem, the double greed, into the normal form required by the TRANSCEND method, the diagram. Something is in the way: scarcity. They have dilemmas, and a classical solution is to give something up, perhaps most of it, 'you cannot have everything in life'. Not much wisdom in that saying. Rather, it sounds like rich people talking to the poor in order to keep them satisfied with little, not too greedy, or like the poor talking to themselves for the same reason.

Apart from the problematic infidelity there is nothing in the goals of the woman and the man excluding each other in anything like a logical sense. The man is more egoistic, I–me–mine; the woman has more solidarity with children and 'others', we–us–ours. But, by and large, they are similar. The 'inner life' is partly New Age, partly as old as the hills. That's not to belittle it. And the example from California above shows that there is no absolute, context-independent conflict between a rich outer and a rich inner life.

The problem lies rather in the relationship between all these goals and something we generally call resources. *Money* is one: travel and art can be money-intensive. *Time* is another: both outer and inner life can be time-consuming. *Energy* is a third: are you sure you can cope? *Ability in self-administration* is a fourth. And here there are some small words which for the most part start with 'wh' that have to be answered: what, why, how, where, when, with whom, and sometimes often against whom, and that's where conflict enters. We are talking about lifestyle, and that is a chain of outer and inner actions, weaving through all these small words that taken singly look so innocent. A rich life demands quite a lot of us, and a soft, mild, administrative capacity to discipline the queue of goals so that they do not gang up against the defences in our soul, conquering us, turning us into a wasteland.

This is where the main problem lies. It is psychological and located in our limited psychological capacity. The goals are lining up. But the purpose is satisfaction, even enrichment, not only to have done it, to have been there, to have seen it. If the goal is a photo-opportunity with travel companions, with the Eiffel Tower as a backdrop, then a photo gives satisfaction. If the goal is to enjoy the Eiffel Tower, the construction, the view, the food in the restaurant high up in the tower – well in that case photography may even stand in the way, blocking the goal.

That is also true here: the goals may be blocking each other, reducing the enjoyment of each one. Formulated this way we end up with a choice between the number of goals on the one hand, and a degree of satisfaction on the other. We give up some goals and enjoy those that are left even more. Live in the present.

Wrong! Indian wisdom declares: this contradiction can be overcome by introducing a forgotten dimension: time. Not the point in time for enjoyment, *kairos,* but the flow of time through life, *chronos* as an agenda, a diary, a plan for the month, the year, a life plan. The Indian rule divides life into four phases *dharma, artha, kama, moksha,* and life focuses on one goal after the other: morals/knowledge, economic activity, enjoyment, and wisdom/liberation. That wisdom is then shared with the children. In the West we also have four phases, childhood–education–work–retirement, CEWR. C and R come with no particular duties and are enjoyment-oriented, but with very little sharing of wisdom in the R phase. Over and out.

Two Hindu rules for living are now regulating the goal queue, dispersing the goals over time:

Always have all four goals in mind as guides to your life, not just one of them. If you seek only one of them you will not achieve even that. They are interlinked.
Without losing any goal from view change the point of gravity through your life from phase to phase, from dharma to artha to kama to moksha.

Never all of them, never only one of them. That's not a bad formula for happiness. And that became the goal for both, in addition to not standing in the way of the happiness of each other and others.

FREUD AND LIFE AS TRANSCENDENCE

We have now looked at some conflicts 'within, and between, persons'. Taking a closer look we see that they are all of both kinds. The parties have their goals, but they are living so tightly together that they also have awareness of the goals of the Other. Even if they are single-mindedly pursuing their own goals they are not blind to the Other.

That brings us to Sigmund Freud. Our goal here is to explore what he really intended to say. Our goal is to confront the best known of all his figures of thought, the struggle between Superego and Id, between Culture/Structure and Nature – the Other in ourselves – with the diagram.

Along one of the axes we have the demands of society, through the norms of the Culture and the constraints put by the Structure, the social tissue. They direct the person in certain directions and away from others. And along the other axis we have the biologically rooted, basic needs, 'the drives', Nature, pressing on. In itself that's not a very original image. Religions are usually based on the struggle between good and evil, with reward for whoever is on the good side, and punishment for whoever yields to evil. The narrow and the broad road, in other words. God and Satan are other names; Freud refers to them as the Superego and Id.

But Freud is not hostile to the drives or unconditionally accepting of 'society', the commandments, the norms. A basic pointer in his teachings is the consequence of letting the Superego dominate the Id beyond breaking point. Among the bourgeoisie of Vienna his focus was on suppressing sexuality; not what happens at the bottom of society when an unemployed person in deep misery fails to steal a highly stealable piece of bread and dies of hunger. Freud would have gone further if he had applied his genius to the whole spectrum of basic needs. Thus, what happens to a nun who gives herself to God and refrains from sexuality, from childbirth and lactation? Or to a woman in general who refrains from childbirth or lactation?

As usual the extreme positions are clear. A human without any drives is as rare as a human with no limits and controls. We may find approximations to the first in some monasteries and to the second under plunder. But then the objection might be that the asceticism in a monastery can develop into a need, and that plundering is also regulated by norms of revenge, and not only by drives. Such extremes in human behaviour are given niches in space for the former and niches in time for the latter. If they were practised everywhere and at all times they would negate human life. The past and the present are eliminated by plunder. And monasteries for all make the future childless.

Withdrawal from both drives and norms carries a name: *death*. Even if the human body technically were kept alive, it would function at a lower level than a vegetable. A newborn baby is something quite different, filled with needs, and the norms are slowly built into the baby by tying them to the satisfaction of those needs.

Compromise is the life most of us are living, with oscillations in the direction of the extreme points. Reasonably norm-obedient, reasonably drive-obedient. Over time a pattern develops, the personality that Freud refers to as Ego, the I. Behaviour has become a habit. When deviating, some warning signs will be flashing: 'exciting, but dangerous' 'correct, but boring'. The variations will derive from shifting attention to the two signals.

But what about *transcendence*? I do not think Freud has any answer. The Id–Superego contradiction has value in itself, a contradiction with which we can live, a struggle that can make us grow. Rich and enriching lives is the goal of this growth, with a reasonable Ego having a reasonable relationship to both soul and body. In love and solidarity with fellow humans. The process is the goal. We all have to find our answers and learn from each other. And Nietzsche's *Übermensch*, Superman, a super-superego beyond good and evil, transcending all norms prescribed for ordinary human beings (or for ordinary nations), is no valid answer. Indeed.

Tuesday: Meso-Conflicts Within Societies

We now proceed from the micro to the meso, from the personal to the social, from psychology to sociology, economics, social philosophy, politics.

What does that mean? We are still dealing with human beings. 'Race' and 'class', economic and political 'forces', defence, school and health 'alternatives', 'gender', are all social constructions. The eight contradictions to be explored are also dividing lines, even fault lines, in society. What does a theory of conflict, worthy of its name, have to contribute?

Our focus is no longer on individual persons and their contradictions, but on categories, groups of persons, and their contradictions with other groups. We have some ideas about what they are and how they relate to other groups. We say about individuals, 'You belong to that group, you to this group', and we attribute to them certain characteristics. We engage in abstractions and generalisations. And we dehumanise. Somewhere at a distance – and let it stay there – genocide looms, defined as *massive category killing,* as a threatening possibility.

But we also generalise about the personal. Psychologists have descriptions of personalities and impose them on concrete persons. Can we live without generalisations, about ourselves, about others, about the weather?

The solution lies in dialogue as a way of penetrating deeper into conflict. Dialogue is with persons, not with categories. We dehumanise the personal Thou by seeing that individual as a representative of a category, of an It. And does that change the I–Thou relation in a dialogue to an I–It relation? The answer is to have many I–Thou dialogues, to be open both to what they have in common and to personal variations. Taken together this may indicate some solutions, as we shall see.

Let us now look at the eight social contradictions. The points of departure are clear, well-known positions. Our task is to explore what the peace diagonal can offer of transcendence and transformation.

THE COLOUR-BLIND SCHOOL

The year was 1958 and the situation was tense to the point of exploding in Charlottesville, Virginia, Thomas Jefferson's home town, in his day a symbol of the new, independent USA. The Supreme Court had, on 17 May 1954, decided that segregated schools for white and coloured students could never be equal, and had ordered the integration of schools in the South 'with all deliberate speed'. What 'deliberate' in this context meant divided the population into three groups, essentially with the following goals:

African Americans: The Supreme Court decision is the law of the land, integrate!

White integrationists: The Supreme Court decision is the law of the land, integrate!

White segregationists: Not here, not now, not in this way: we are not ready!

So this was a conflict with three parties and two goals, and with a large majority sitting on the fence, as usual, waiting. The white people were organised in a 'Human Relations Council' and a 'White Citizens Council for State Rights and Individual Liberties'; the former to create more closeness, the latter to maintain distance, remoteness, and to delay the inevitable as long as possible.

But there was also another difference between the two white groups. The integrationists were often immigrants from the North, intellectuals without local roots. The segregationists were farmers and working people who had lived in the South for generations. From their point of view the town was theirs, the integrationists were immigrants, and the coloured people who once had been necessary were now considered an unnecessary, and partly dangerous, evil.

There was one important exception: Sara Patton Boyle, an FFV (First Families of Virginia), with impeccable credentials as a genuine child of that state. None the less, she was a super-active integrationist. Outside her window one night the Ku Klux Klan burnt a cross as a warning. There was a dark thundercloud of violence hanging over the conflict.

There were very strong emotions and memories of slavery and mutiny, of civil war, victory and defeat.

The segregationists hated the idea that they might lose the civil war once again, and they fought with lawyers using all kind of stratagems against the inevitable, partly not to capitulate without having put up a fight.

The integrationists tried, not without problems, to become a good model for black–white relations, thereby showing others that there was nothing to fear from proximity. Nobody dared to say anything publicly lest that could unleash a violent reaction. The position of the segregationists was illegitimate, even illegal after the Supreme Court decision. Defiance could trigger federal action. The position of the others was legitimate, even legal, but could trigger violence from below. It was all about black people, but they had no power one way or the other. Locally, they were waiting. They were well organised from New York (National Association for the Advancement of Colored People, NAACP) and Atlanta, Georgia (Southern Leadership Conference, SLC). All of them had been waiting. The Supreme Court had also been waiting, for years. And now they were suddenly forced to express their position in action. There was some talk about compromise: take the universities first, then the rest; start where 'conditions are right', then the rest. That could easily take generations.

The segregationists were the ones who invented a transcendence, and a non-violent one at that: they organised private schools rather than 'exposing their children to miscegenation' in state-funded schools. This was only for those who had enough money and a sustainable racism. The others, less well off and less firm in their racist creed, bowed to the inevitable.

The contribution of this author was to make the groups visible to each other, and through public opinion polls show that people regarded integration as inevitable, that nobody wanted violence, and that the private schools were a feasible, if temporary, solution.

Solutions can sometimes come from unexpected quarters. The segregationists had been regarded as super-rigid, totally unwilling to yield. But they transcended the conflict by bringing in a new social reality: private schools.

We may question how successful this was. This alternative loomed more and more in the US debate and in US reality. The well-off are not only placing their children outside state-funded schools, but also demand the education component of the tax they pay as vouchers, coupons, that can be redeemed in private schools.

On French railway crossings there is often a warning sign: '*Un train peut en cacher un autre*', 'One train can hide another'. One train is coming from the right, passing, but masking the train coming from the left. The pleasure of crossing quickly because the train from the right has just passed can be of rather short duration.

A conflict can hide another following in its wake. One reaction can be 'Let's face the new conflict when we come to it. We cannot postpone transcendence/transformation of one conflict because another may be following it.' If we become obsessed with society as a strongly coupled machinery, then we will either become too paralysed to touch ('tinker with') it, or say 'First we have to clean up everything from the bottom'. And we can't do that, or lack the courage to do it. The result may well be that nothing is done. Better be aware of the danger and try to engage in some prophylaxis without becoming too paralysed, like communists/Christians waiting for world revolution/the Messiah.

Charlottesville suffered from 'pluralistic ignorance', ignorance about the real attitudes of the people, and an exaggerated fear. Public opinion data made available by the author about the divided but essentially peaceful population encouraged desegregation. Data about hatred and preparation for violence would have led to counter-measures and possibly to violence.

THE CLASSLESS COMPANY

The scene is a classic class conflict. A small company with an owner and a worker, that is all. The means of production are owned by the owner, and the worker is paid from the income from the sale of the products. The problem is that the working conditions are miserable: a draughty room with bad odours and dangerous toxins. Lungs are exposed to poisonous gases and cold, humid air. The worker is in bad shape. But when he calls in sick work comes to a halt, the revenue goes down and that is the basis for a miserable salary. Still, better than no salary at all.

The Worker: The working conditions are scandalous; if I don't get decent ventilation and the holes and cracks in the wall are not fixed, then I will go on strike and will warn everybody else against working under such conditions!

The Owner: Here are the orders we have received, and our accounts. The answer is obvious: there is not enough money for the necessary repairs!

Many workers have heard a similar tale over the years. And sometimes it might be true. The contradiction between the owner who does not want to improve the working conditions and the worker who wants to change them is built into the system. That conflict can be transcended negatively by closing the company; neither worker nor owner will get anything. And victory for one is obviously defeat for the other. There was no space for compromise: the owner could have done some little thing, and the worker could accept that 'thing' in the short term. But by this point compromise had been rejected by both as too little for one and too expensive for the other.

The strike was imminent, and with that closure of the company; in other words, considerably more than the lock-out of one worker. The end.

There is urgency about transcendence, not only for those two but also for the third party, the customers, and the fourth party, the suppliers. Could the key to transcendence be located in any one of them?

The conflict worker talks with all four parties and finds that all of them have a strong interest in keeping the company going, but not strong enough to raise a loan. The worker understands too little of how a company is run, and the owner knows too little about the job the worker does and its associated problems. In spite of the minimal size of the company they are living in two different worlds.

Transcendence: The distinction between worker and owner is abolished by having both entering the company as equals, by turning the company into a cooperative. The former owner will spend four days a week on the machines and will acquire an increased understanding, including physically, of the implications of the job in terms of odours and draught. The former worker will spend one day a week in the office and learn how little he understands of reliable supply, loyal work and buyers creating enough cash flow to pay for the other two, plus a little profit. He will also understand that there is not enough work for a full-time employee in the office after the company has invested in a course in bookkeeping for him, and in technology for the former owner. In other words, the company is in for reorganisation, eight days on the floor and two in the office each five-day week, against the previous five plus five. Result: a considerable increase in productivity and production, and material flow in one direction and cash flow in the other.

Conflict will not always find such a successful positive transcendence, and the former owner may use his new position to buy out the former worker when profitability improves. Perhaps this is more easily done in small companies. But making the borders in the economic cycle more penetrable is a good general formula for a better flow in the cycle, and through that for transformation of conflicts along that cycle in general.

ECONOMIC ALTERNATIVES

Let us now take a look at the big economic debate and struggle that has put its stamp on the past century and is going to re-emerge fully in the present one. Should the ownership of the means of production and finance be private, individual or collective (as in a cooperative), or should it be public, in the hands of the state? Ownership includes the right to decide where and how these goods are made use of in the economic cycle from raw materials via production to consumption. The owner has some resources. How and where is he going to invest them? Will he let the market decide, finding the path to maximum *profit*, whether in the productive economy or in the finance economy? Or, should he let *basic human needs*, individual and/or collective, decide?

The debate is well known, perhaps even tinged with boredom. Nevertheless, or precisely for that reason, it is interesting to see how primitive this debate actually was, and how a little use of the diagram can give new perspectives on the transformation of economic conflicts.

Let us first note that the problem of ownership is not the same as the problem of running the company. Of course, the private owner can make plans putting human needs at the centre, not only demand. And the state can also run a company where profit is in focus. But usually the state legitimises itself in terms of an orientation towards basic needs and welfare for all, and the private sector enjoys a guarantee – presumably given by Adam Smith – that their selfish profit orientation will be in the interest of everybody, that one million egoisms = altruism, and more so than if basic needs had been the focus.

Let us now simplify this to *private–market–profit,* in conflict with *state–plan–needs.* The positions of the two parties are formulated above. We are talking about what are called right-wing and left-wing forces, to employ somewhat tired words. But they are concrete human beings made of flesh and blood. Meso-conflicts easily spill over into micro-conflicts.

Is this a bit old-fashioned? Perhaps. But if somebody usurps right-wing ideology, fighting for private–market–profit with the hope that a highly reduced state will still be able to steer profit in the direction of basic needs, and refers to this as the 'Third Way', then a number of formerly left-wing parties have transformed themselves into right-wing parties. What they do is what counts, not what they call themselves. By hijacking the programmes of right-wing parties they have also hijacked the voters from these parties and made them programme-less, at least until they start thinking independently. The democratic debate is not benefiting from a narrowing of the political spectrum. Better to breathe new life into what is 'old-fashioned'.

The twentieth century witnessed a political pendulum swinging along the bi-diagonal, from market to plan, via the social democratic mixed-economy compromise, and then back again. And then possibly back again. But these are only three of the five positions. What happened to negative and positive transcendence? And what kind of pauper's diet is this, a menu with only three of the five courses?

The unit of economic policy constructed in the twentieth century was national, regional or even global (in the 1990s), meaning that withdrawal from the conflict would imply local economies. In other words, traditional village economics. Withdrawal = turning back the clock of history? Well, why not? It may be rational to turn back the clock when we are in another time zone; maybe that is exactly where we are. But the point is not to argue, but to make the missing two positions in the debate meaningful, both verbally and conceptually.

But this is still begging the question, what is positive transcendence, both/and? The best empirical examples are probably the Japanese and East Asian economies before the USA insisted on reorganisation, meaning unambiguous change in the direction of private–market–profit. That wave is now found all over the world under the rubric 'privatisation'; in other words, one of the two extremist positions.

The Japanese both/and was a market economy micro-controlled by the state through planning and incentives. The market had the final say in the domestic economic cycle; the state in the world market. The basic needs of the workers were taken care of by both. It is indisputable that micro-control and subsidy/incentives sometimes went too far. Much that would not have survived in a purely competitive market economy was kept artificially alive. But the system was able to satisfy basic needs better than a purely market-oriented economy and created more economic growth than a purely plan-oriented economy. A Soviet economist once said to this author: 'These damned Japanese capitalists are better at economic planning than we are.' And he or his US colleagues could have added: 'These damned Japanese socialists are better at market economics than we are.' In 2003 it didn't look like that. Let us have another look in a few years' time when Japan has found a way back to its former self.

So we land on the main diagonal, [3] + [4] + [5], away from the extreme positions Market and Plan as a better three-course menu for conflict transformation. In other words, a complex, mixed economy.

That economy would include a traditional *local sector*, particularly for basic needs, food (with fresh air and water), housing and clothing, basic health (local clinics), basic education, for instance as education cafeterias tied to the internet as schools in the classic sense will probably slowly disappear. Much of this would be exchange- rather than money-based, and if money-based, then often in a local, not national, currency.

The *national sector* could be a mixed economy of a social democratic type, producing means of production, and of consumption, for domestic demand.

The third component could be a both/and sector at a high level, and like the classic Japanese pattern would aim at export in the *global economy* (see *Peace by Peaceful Means*, part III).

And the conflict transformation would be the combination of all three.

POLITICAL ALTERNATIVES

Let us take a look at what this approach to conflict carries in its wake for political systems, 'polities', like 'economies' always in plural.

Today many are of the opinion that the debate and struggle between Market and Plan was won by Market. If these are the only alternatives available on the hard disk of the brain, and they are referred to as 'capitalism' and 'socialism', this might be the correct conclusion, right now. If we include the other three possibilities, it becomes more complicated.

The contradiction between democracy and dictatorship, however, was clearly won by democracy. *Dictatorship is illegitimate.* In practice we still have gender-, generation-, race-, class- and nation-based dictatorships, but nobody comes to their defence. Patriarchs, old men, prefer silence. The same applies to racism, which once was at the root of colonialism. The 'dictatorship of the proletariat' also has few defenders today in spite of the fact that the 'dictatorship of the bourgeoisie' is still widespread. And even if almost all multinational states are ruled by one dominant nation, very few would defend this as a principle except for Jews, in the Jewish state of Israel.

But let us confront 'polities' with the diagram and as before see if the peace diagonal could have something interesting to offer because even within 'democracy' there are different positions and deep contradictions.

The extreme positions are clear: democracy means *rule by everybody*, and dictatorship is *rule by somebody*, more precisely one body, usually a man. That they exclude each other seems obvious. But there is actually an historically important positive transcendence, rule by one person who is seen as an *incarnation of the collective will*, '*la volonté générale*', the one person to whom people are willing to give all their power, the one they will follow through fire and water. That was Nelson Mandela when apartheid came to an end, Kwame Nkrumah when colonialism had come to an end, perhaps Napoleon Bonaparte when the Terror had come to an end. But watch out: the mandate can be withdrawn. Of the three, only Mandela understood that there was a time limit.

The most important approximation today to democracy as 'rule by everybody' is the Swiss *direct democracy*, not only via referendums but also via initiatives in the sense that the citizens by signing a petition can demand a referendum. In other democracies we are dealing with compromises. There is a vote over the general course of the polity, with solutions presented in packages called party manifestos. But that vote takes place only once every four years or so. A window is opened for a day or two and is referred to as an 'election'. The details are left to an oligarchy, a rule by several bodies such as political parties, often referred to as 'the political class', or 'caste' when it is particularly self-recruiting. This election of a political class is what we have in *indirect democracy*, which for that reason is better referred to by its correct, if less attractive, name: *parliamentocracy*. But even in direct democracies it can be made more direct through referendums, particularly at the local level.

Dictatorship is excluded from our considerations, being illegitimate. But all the others are on a rich democratic menu, as opposed to the poor, two-course menu of dictatorship-and-democracy. The question is, what kind of democracy?

Democracy with all power given to one person who enjoys everybody's confidence may be important in times of crisis. Norway occupied by Nazi Germany did not have such a figure. The King came closest, but did not have the mandate. There was an exiled prime minister who had the mandate, but was not the person. There was an opposition politician who came closer, but did not have the mandate. Vidkun Quisling had the power, but certainly not the mandate. He looked at that power as a means to go beyond the traditional norms of democracy, creating his own norms as legitimation. The Führer principle, in other words, in the shadow of Nietzsche.

The last possibility, neither democracy nor dictatorship, is usually referred to as *anarchy*. The political structure is suspended. The tissue becomes very thin to the point of collapse, and what is left are cultural norms and basic needs. If the norms are also suspended, this is referred to as *anomie*. We are left with basic needs and an egoistic cost-benefit analysis. Postmodern society?

What we are aiming at, as with 'economic alternatives', is to show what we can get out of the basic diagram. Where there are two forces directed against each other, democracy and dictatorship, there will always be five possibilities, not two. We get an impoverished, even moronic debate by reducing this to 'democracy versus dictatorship' or 'capitalism versus socialism'. There is much more to be found under the sun, like incarnation democracy, direct democracy, indirect democracy and anarchy. They can be combined in ways that better reflect what we had in the past, not to mention what we may get in the future.

The problem may be deep cultures that hate the number 5 and love the number 2. Such deep cultures are called dualistic, permitting only two categories – right–wrong, good–bad. This is certainly the case for much of our Western culture, and more particularly for US and Russian culture.

Thus, a typical American way of expressing this would be that there were once two political systems, dictatorship and democracy, and democracy won. There were once two economic systems, socialism and capitalism, and capitalism won. The former happened after the Second World War, the latter after the Cold War. But that's much too simplistic.

The End of History, by Francis Fukuyama, former deputy head of the planning section in the US State Department, concluded, like Marx and Engels, that the pre-history of humankind will come to an end and that real history will be based on electoral democracy and market liberalism. Using dualism as a guide it may look like that. The number '5' is not very high either, but it opens up considerably more possibilities than that thought prison, the number '2'. For Mikhail Gorbachev it must have been almost impossible to explain to the Russian people the meaning of 'social democracy'. He represented much of that before he was removed and is still chair of a small party with that name. But the Russians also thought in two categories and came to the same conclusions as the Americans: if socialism was wrong, then capitalism has to be valid as there are only two categories. The basic problem is located in deep culture, so that is where it must be solved.

Why is democracy so problematic in the third world? Why are there so many coups and counter-coups? There are many explanations, but one stands out as potentially particularly convincing. Democracy in general, and elections in particular, are a part of the theory of the state. It is a question of who for a limited period of time – four years, eight years – is going to administer the rewards of the state, have access to housing for ministers, cars, fix tax rates and customs and excise duties, control natural resources and the possibility of selling access to them to foreign firms in return for bribes. Add to this the control of the military and police. The poorer the people, the more this must look like paradise on earth, an inexhaustible resource. And all for oneself, as the politician elected by the people.

The incumbent government can use the resources of the state to buy votes. The opposition knows about this and organises a coup to 'cleanse the country of corruption'. They now have the problem that they also want better access to the pork barrel and to democratic legitimacy. The way ahead passes through the presentation of themselves as the saviours of the country, those who really wanted to clean up everything – and then commit the same crimes until the next generation of saviours comes forward, with the same legitimation.

How are coups avoided? Rich countries have their methods. Those who are elected get sufficient recompense to perform their legislative, executive or judiciary duties, but not so much that these rewards become a motive in their own right. In poor countries the average salary will not be sufficient to exercise such duties and in addition carry out tasks of representation. The answer is not that it costs much less to pay a single dictator than a whole democratically elected political class. The answer is democracy.

Even more democracy. But without too many rewards at the top. How? By making the pyramid flatter, decentralising the state, offering more power to the local levels, fewer rewards for the elected people's representatives. And at the same time leave more decisions to be made by the people themselves, in local and national referendums.

Some years ago I was standing in the town square of Lillehammer, in Norway, listening to two prime ministerial candidates in the forthcoming election, two skilful, experienced politicians setting out their positions and also emphasising their disagreements. This was probably also true for me; I was mainly thinking of the many things with which I disagreed. As they were basically in agreement about Norwegian foreign policy, that aspect of politics was unmentioned. And as the voters tend to form their opinions around issues of disagreement the net result is the depoliticisation of foreign policy. 'Foreign policy above the parties' they call it.

Imagine now that instead of debating, trying to defeat each other with words, they had used their eloquence in a dialogue, with the aim of finding how their contradictions could be transcended and their perspectives combined in a higher unity. What they stood for was never so wrong that there was nothing good in it, but perhaps not so good either that there was nothing wrong with it. In other words, if they had complemented rather than contradicted each other they could have lifted Norway higher instead of letting the country swing like a pendulum between two known positions. But for that to happen the strong points in the antagonist had to be seen as possible remedies for one's own weakness. Problematic?

The voters could demand searching, transcending dialogues rather than dog fights, and then vote for the candidate more able to learn from his own antagonist = counterpart. In Australia there are movements encouraging Australian voters to do exactly that.

Dialogue democracy rather than debate democracy. My thoughts went to the great mathematician David Hilbert, who once said that human beings have a more or less broad horizon. With some people this horizon shrinks to one single point, which they refer to as their point of view. Perhaps some joint work to expand that horizon would benefit democracy better than a parade of positions, viewpoints. The government would in that case be a coalition, centred on the dialogue. Why not?

DEFENCE ALTERNATIVES

The time has come for security politics. States, nations and other groups attack one another, sometimes by violent means, from fists to the threat of nuclear bombs, and cause traumas to the body, mind and spirit. The means to prevent this are referred to as *defence*. The question is how, and that leads to well-known conflicts over security. Let us try some transformation of that conflict as it is expressed in debates about defence, and see how far we can come.

The extremist positions in a traditional defence debate are:

Purely military defence: By violent means, to destroy the machinery of destruction held by the other side. There are four approaches, military doctrines:

(1) Offensive offence, without any solid grounds for suspicion, simply because 'he is evil'.
(2) Defensive offence, preventive war, cutting him off.
(3) Offensive defence, responding to his attack, on his own turf.
(4) Defensive defence, engage in the war, but on our own turf.

Problem: offensive offence, defensive offence and offensive defence all presuppose long-distance weapons capable of operating within the territory of the enemy, and the existence of such weapons can be seen as a provocation, regardless of the intention, and trigger the attack they were supposed to prevent.

Purely non-violent defence: By non-violent means, in order to deprive the other party of the fruits of an attack. There are three basic approaches:

(i) Non-cooperation and civil disobedience, including sabotage of infrastructure in order to deprive him of social, economic and political goals.
(ii) Make oneself as invulnerable as possible, building horizontal networks, storing foods, medicine, etc.; in short being well prepared.
(iii) Never hurt or harm the other side, but meet him as one human being meeting another, be friendly, in dialogue, but determined where non-cooperation is concerned.

The extreme positions would assert and practise one and only one of these two alternatives. The former, purely military defence, today prevails in about 170 of the countries of the world. Thirty countries have no army; in other words, they have 'withdrawn' from the problem because they do not have any non-violent defence either. About half of these have a defence agreement with another country. The latter, purely non-violent defence, is found in no country. In other words, only two of the five outcome possibilities have been tried.

Here we will concentrate on compromise and transcendence. Compromise is also known as a 'combi-defence'; military at the border, and if that is not sufficient to stop an attack, then non-military defence takes over inside the country. And if that is not sufficient, the other side has won.

To get a twist on this dilemma, which has generated strong verbal strife between those who stand for the military and the pacifists, we have to look at positions that are located more deeply. The Swiss psychologist Jean Piaget makes a distinction between absolutism and reciprocity, personified here as The Absolute and The Reciprocal, as two ways of seeing the Other, well known from class struggle, gender struggle, the Cold War, from USA/West against the Rest of the World after the 11 September terror in New York and Washington, and so on. Or from any violent conflict.

The Absolute looks at the antagonist as simply unconditionally evil. What we have done has nothing to do with it. In his malice he will make use of any weaknesses we might have to exercise evil. The only way out is to incapacitate him by using doctrines (1)–(4), particularly (1) and (2).

The Reciprocal, who's more mature, will ask himself if there is something we have done that could have made the Other so violent, and something we can do (or rather undo) to make him less violent: a friendly attitude, letting him talk, listening to his side of the story. In short, dialogue rather than debate, which easily becomes a continuation of war by verbal means. A dialogue of this kind where all parties can speak their minds and formulate their goals could, possibly, lead to a conflict transformation if the contradictions could be transcended. If violence has taken place, then reconciliation is also needed, a process even more complex than conflict transformation.

But some defence is also necessary. The problem arises when (1), (2) and (3) provoke because the offensive parts of the machinery can also be used to attack. That leads to (4) as a defence doctrine: in other words, to conventional, short-distance defence, and/or to a militia/guerrilla warfare. And added to that non-violent defence, all three of them together, (i), (ii) and (iii).

A country of that kind would have a triple force to rely on. If one of them fails, then there are still two reliable legs to walk on for some time, with no victory/defeat in sight. The basic problem is not defence policy, but rather a deep culture which pulls in the direction of absolutism and away from reciprocity, and militarism *or* pacifism, no both/and. That will be the theme on Friday.

SCHOOLS AND ALTERNATIVE SCHOOLS

Student A, bully: I hate school. Training, discipline, being forced. I am suffering, bored to death. I'd like to burn down the whole lot, with some of the worst teachers inside.

Student B, victim: I love school. I am learning so much, every day, languages, history, mathematics. If it wasn't for A who is always tormenting me. He cannot stand anybody simply liking school.

Conflict Worker: Is that right, A, you attack B because he likes what you loathe? The school is so strong, you don't dare hit that, so you hit B instead. He cannot hit back and you know it!

Student A, bully: Say what you like. I am not going to hate this school less for that reason. Go ahead with your analysis, just go ahead!

Conflict Worker: So, what are we doing here? The example is from Japan, but the phenomenon is global. What happens is that the bullies are studied and punished, their victims are studied and assisted, the relationship between the two is studied and improved. 'The school system', 'society' (meaning the elites) usually prefer a bully-oriented, iron-clad, 'zero tolerance' approach. A primitive, immature individualisation of a rather deep problem.

The statements point to the school itself as a problem. A traditional school suits B very well. A finds himself an unskilled job, joins a motorbike gang and becomes a dropout. A tough teacher will leave A to his punishment. A soft teacher will call a class meeting and start mediating between A and B. But all of this has one thing in common: the focus is not on the school. The focus is on A and B.

So let us start with a first jump: instead of looking at A and B as perpetrator and victim, a perspective that also will be needed, let us look at them as two school politicians.

A is right: the school is disciplinary, instilling respect for *space* (buildings, classroom, desk), *time* (the hour, the minutes in between) and *authority* (teacher, authorities, school curriculum). What is being taught usually coincides with the ideology of men, more particularly dead white men, the upper and middle classes, and the dominant nation. A lack of choice spells authoritarianism. The result has been a plethora of alternative schools.

But B is also right: many are thriving in the school just as it is.

A seems to want a school with more freedom of choice, not only where knowledge and skills are concerned, but also as to where, when and how. B seems to want clear guidelines, both as to content and where–when–how. An alternative school for A with a course in repairing motorbikes, and a traditional school for B? But will the conflict really be solved when both have their goals satisfied? Isn't that a bit like the couple flying separately, or the siesta for the husband in the bedroom and fiesta for the wife in the living room? We make the conflict too easy if we disregard the *link* between the parties, the idea of being together.

We are looking for one school where both can feel at home, not a traditional school for B and a special school for A. We want positive transcendence, not a compromise, or a negative transcendence eliminating all schools.

Weak positive transcendence would give them a voucher which they could redeem at different schools, according to their choice, as they are floating through the *chronos* of the school years, quickly for some, slowly as if through treacle for others, who are longing for the end to this publicly financed torture. A year at a different kind of school abroad is generally recognised. Why not a year at a different kind of school in one's own country, even one's own town?

Strong positive transcendence would build more types of schools (traditional, Steiner/Waldorf, experimental in general) in the same school building and then let them blossom together, let the students select their classes and decide themselves whether they want to stay or continue searching. Of course, this can become restless. But the honey bee flying from flower to flower is sucking nectar from a number of places and may fertilise even more the more chaotic the itinerary. A ministry for honey bees would probably authorise only one standard itinerary for all bees. But perhaps the bee can learn better by finding out for itself?

The problem is the either/or of the debating culture. A more pluralistic society would have used the both/and of dialogue cultures to let human diversity be mirrored in social diversity. The universities are well in advance in this regard, permitting students much leeway in planning their curriculum. It is high time that schools followed suit.

SCHOOL MEDICINE AND ALTERNATIVE MEDICINE

The health debate reminds us of the school debate. The generally recognised institution for education is known as a *school*; the generally recognised approach to health is known as *school medicine*. It is being taught in medical schools and confers a licence to practise health work. The alternative is usually referred to as *alternative medicine*.

Conflict Worker: Again the problem is to get hold of the contradiction between school medicine and alternative medicine. Both have health as their goal even if the definitions are somewhat different. They both make use of diagnosis–prognosis–therapy as a schema. Both are of the opinion that the patient has to have health as his goal, be cooperative and work to obtain this (a basic article of faith, particularly among alternative practitioners). School medicine is still tied to thinking in terms of cases and looks at the patient more as a case bearing a bundle of symptoms. The alternative practitioners focus more on the whole person and on the context.

School Medicine:
The parts: The organism is a system of organs and functions, and the therapy has to be precise and aim at specific organs and functions.
Irreversibility: Where nature proves insufficient the therapy will consist in precise surgical intervention, using chemotherapy, etc. and modern science in general in order to assist nature. We are not afraid of doing something irreversible.
Evaluation: Therapy X shall focus on the bundle of symptoms Y, and be evaluated by checking to what extent X has any effect on Y.

Alternative Medicine:
The totality: Body, mind, spirit and context are a unity, they are strongly linked. Diagnosis, prognosis and therapy have to encompass all of them with the patient reporting his own suffering, in context. The totality is what matters.
Reversibility: An intervention has to be multi-dimensional, soft and not expose the patient to anything irreversible, partly because we can make mistakes, partly because of the couplings in a holistic organism,

and partly to stimulate the complex self-healing capacity of any human being.

Evaluation: A therapy can have a focus but shall work holistically; for that reason the evaluation will have to span many fields.

School Medicine: The specific, the concrete is what makes us scientific, whereas you are talking and acting only in general, without any precision.

Alternative Medicine: The many dimensional approach is indispensable for true and sustainable health, whereas you are only fixing a little point or two.

In other words, we are dealing with basic differences, not only in how to act but also how to think. The evaluation will have to be adjusted to these differences. Conclusions will tend to be different because the point of departure is so different.

As we are dealing with a central value, health, close to life itself and for that reason to 'higher forces', the use of language will often become very strong. School medicine sees alternative practitioners as 'quacks'; they in turn see school medicine as driven by power and profit. School medicine is seeking power by controlling health, and profit by selling expensive unnatural interventions, working against the self-healing forces of nature. It has the support of the state and the pharmaceutical industry in a triangular cooperation, and easily forgets that they were once an alternative.

Victory can lead to monopoly. School medicine is close to this and many alternative practitioners may want it too. This is a struggle over such scarce means as access to patients and through that to honoraria, directly or through the social security system, and to be licensed, among other things to get access to social security funding. The compromise would consist in school medicine yielding some of its monopoly, and giving it to the alternative practitioners. As for schools this will probably function mostly for national groups who can claim that their medical practice is a part of their national culture. The result would be parallel health systems within, not only between, countries.

But this is not transcendence. No new social reality has been created, only two parallel, coexisting realities. Transcendence would, as for schools, consist in giving patients a totally free choice, then building the two forms or approaches into the same clinic and hospital, and integrating them through overarching perspectives, all the time maintaining the patient's freedom of choice. In the longer run physicians should be trained in both. On the road to this it might be interesting to subject both to the evaluation procedure of the other. Why not?

We are moving in that direction. But either/or is still stronger than both/and.

WOMEN, MEN AND THE GOOD SOCIETY

Let us now turn to the gender conflict. 'Men and women, He created them.' But Genesis is more about contradiction than about love. The question is how we can reformulate the contradiction between women and men, in the plural this time, if acted out in countless micro-level conflicts. Love, and the contradiction between one man and one woman, is probably the most frequent theme in world literature. And the contradiction woman/man in general has become more salient as an axis for social analysis in a number of countries than even class. The power of patriarchy over women has now been made visible, just as Marx once did for the power of the bourgeoisie over the proletariat. But from that it doesn't follow that it is simple to verbalise the contradiction between woman and man.

As a point of departure let us note the rough numerical balance, 50/50, and at the same time power imbalance, between the genders. There is a contradiction between numerical balance and power imbalance. But what kind of power are we talking about?

Two interpretations emerge after some reflection. The first is simple, even trivial, but extremely important: the exercise of formal social power; having positions of leadership; recruitment to the social niches leading to power and leadership.

The second interpretation is deeper but more problematic. If we interpret 'women' as 'female', and 'men' as 'male', could this refer to a contradiction between two social cultures? The first interpretation is easy to dress up in numbers and leads us to important tables with the percentage of women and of men along all kinds of dimensions. The second interpretation is not so easily quantified. And many might even object that talking about 'male' and 'female' is 'essentialism', unquantifiable and in addition politically suspect because it generalises about huge categories of human beings, attributing to them permanent properties, with no variation in time and space and from one individual to the other. Essence attribution has a tendency to become normative: depending on whether you are this way or that you are or are not a real woman/man.

We could of course object that this also applies to basic needs, which are seen in this book as inherent characteristics of human beings. And there is no thesis that variation does not exist within the 'female' and the 'male'. As a matter of fact, it would be interesting to know more about how people in general look at the woman/man distinction, and to what extent they see contradictions.

Let us start with the first interpretation, for macro-society. The two extreme positions are well known. They are referred to as patriarchy and matriarchy. The former has a high frequency today, but the latter can also be found in smaller societies, for instance on the southern slopes of the Himalayas.

Conflict Worker: As usual, the main job is to clarify the other three positions. They are more interesting since they can give us more insight. We have to visualise them as clearly as possible, and then squeeze the basic diagram for whatever it is worth.

50/50 is here. That is what everybody talks about, equality. But 0/0 would also be some type of equality, only more original. Dominance by neither men nor women could mean dominance by children and/or by older people. Social power could be given to the sexually less active, so that the active could focus entirely on their games. Negative transcendence, in other words.

But what about positive transcendence? Logically impossible, we cannot possibly give 100 per cent of power to women and at the same time 100 per cent to men.

The answer would as usual be found by differentiating 'power' into components. Thus, it can be argued that in Japan and India men have (almost) all the power in society, and women (almost) all the power in the home, over the family budget (thus, car salesmen there target the woman), family planning, the foreign policy of the family. Matriarchal families within a patriarchal society. And is it so obvious what is more important, macro-society or household society, the *oikos*? What is obvious is that power is many-dimensional, that many societies are patriarchal at both the meso- and micro-levels, and that very few societies are matriarchal at both levels.

We could also imagine the power of macro-society differentiated into ministries with ministers who usually are men or are women, something that already exists. Is this the last barricade of patriarchy? Women are unstoppable, so give them the least important ministries, certainly not foreign affairs and defence. Or is there also the idea that certain sectors of society can be better handled by women? Something related to the old idea of female and male occupations?

That much of this are strategies to maintain patriarchy, 'a hierarchy where men at the top exercise structural and often also direct violence over women at the bottom, legitimated by cultural violence', is hardly in doubt. But perhaps we can also talk about something female/male.

	Female	Male
Value Culture	Basic needs	Abstract values
Motivation Culture	Holistic, empathetic	Specific, deductive
Form of Control	Through closeness, horizontal, non-violent	Through distance, vertical, often violent
Form of Sanction	Love and its absence	Discipline and its absence

There is something about this that leads our thinking towards a division of labour and of roles, more towards the relation between genders than towards absolute, 'essentialist' differences. In other words, towards social structure. At the meso-level changes in the division of labour, where division of roles, are slow. At the micro-level it is simpler for him and her to share: housework, cooking, child care and the family budget are more or less 50/50. The types of education that can produce the differences are indicated in the table, and increased consciousness about such possibilities should be easy. Then society will have to catch up, sooner or later.

But then comes the big question: What happens if we find that 'female' is legitimate, so valid that we want to keep it just as it is and change 'male' in that direction? What happens if 'female' is more, and 'male' less, legitimate? Look at it from the point of view of this book, *An Introduction to Conflict Work*. Much emphasis has been put on *empathy*, not as deep understanding – though that is also important – but as deep feeling, as the ability to feel the feelings of all the parties, their frustration in connection with unobtainable goals, their aggression towards those who stand in the way, their feelings of hopelessness, apathy, powerlessness, their joy when there is a glimmer of light, and their sometimes strong defences against understanding the feelings of the other side. There is a focus on *non-violence*, not only as an abstract rejection of violence, but as a feeling of repulsion and a corresponding joy when there is love, one's own or that of others. And there is much focus on using one's own thinking and that of others to the utmost, with *creativity to arrive at transcendence*, whether negative or positive.

These three are neither specifically female nor specifically male. But the first two demand a strong sense of basic needs and with that a rejection of violence since violence is precisely to insult basic needs; solidarity with all parties; empathy, closeness, love for the repugnant. Let the author generalise only to himself: my concrete experience is that women are far stronger in all of these aspects of being human and for that reason also the better conflict workers.

Conclusion: *let 'female' prevail, let 'male' yield*. A compromise will only dilute the excellent characteristics in the column for female in the table, more right-hand side of the brain, less left-hand. Of course, both genders have potentials in those directions. But a both/and transcendence of the gender contradiction is too egalitarian, too symmetrical. And a neither/nor is tantamount to collective suicide. We will return to this after we have had a look at Marx. Goals can also be illegitimate. In that case, let them be defeated.

SWITZERLAND AS TRANSCENDENCE

Let us now do something totally different; let us use this perspective on conflict to read history backwards, to look at the present as transcendence, and history as the story about which conflicts were the origins for which acceptable and sustainable types of transcendence. We will take Switzerland as our example. We know the result. But what were the problems, the conflicts that gave rise to Switzerland?

High up in the Alps, Europe's water tower, from where water flows into Europe's four principal rivers (the Rhine, the Danube, the Po, the Rhône) three peasant populations were living, not wanting to become the periphery of, respectively, Salzburg/Berlin, Milan and Paris. They found *joint independence*. As Austria/Germany, Italy and France were constantly at war with each other they had to put some constraints on their participation in order not to be torn to pieces by divided loyalties. Warfare became an impossibility and *the first neutral state in the world emerged, Switzerland*.

On the one hand, they wanted to defend their country, on the other, they did not want to provoke their neighbours. So they built a military machinery based on defence inside the country more than just defending the border, and on short-distance more than on long-distance weaponry. In doing so they became the first country with a clearly *defensive defence* as a military doctrine.

In order to root this defence of geographical space locally and reduce the danger of using the army against the people, military service became obligatory and locally based. After four months' training, two weeks' military service a year for twelve years. The soldiers keep their weapons at home with the result that the army was some kind of *class-free militia*.

Nor did they want to be dominated by countries united in a European Union. For that reason no to negotiations for membership; but yes to cooperation within the OSCE, OECD, Council of Europe and the United Nations which either do not demand military duties of them, or are based on consensus, in other words on the possibility of veto.

Nor did they want to become peripheries of each other, particularly not of the German-speaking majority. For that reason they created a system with inner autonomy and coexistence of the language groups (70 per cent German, 25 per cent French, 4 per cent Italian, and 1 per cent for the fourth group, the 'indigenous', Rhetoromanian). Switzerland became *the first multinational country with equality among nations*.

For these groups to remain equal Switzerland was a confederation until 1848, and became a federation from 1874; with joint foreign, security and finance policies, and other policies decided locally.

In Switzerland peasant revolts over the centuries won and led to a tradition of *direct democracy*, based on *referendums*, until recently restricted to men only. Switzerland, with 1 per cent of the world's population, held 60 per cent of the national referendums in the twentieth century.

For democracy to be rooted in the people, the people can also take the initiative for the government to hold a referendum within two years, if 100,000 signatures are raised.

In order for the decisions really to be local the units should not be too big. For that reason Switzerland is not divided into four, but into 23 cantons (three of them divided into half-cantons) – one Rhetoromanian, one Italian, four totally and two partly French. The rest are German-speaking, and partly very small.

In order to avoid one nation dominating the cabinet its seven members do not only represent the parties, but also the four nations (*Zauberformel*, the magical formula). This is actually a permanent coalition government accountable directly to the people rather than to the national assembly it mirrors.

Independence for four rather than just one nation, neutrality, defensive defence, militia, international organisations where neutrals can participate, egalitarian multinationality, confederation, direct democracy, initiative, cantons and the magical formula are Swiss transcendences. An enormous contribution. Thank you, Switzerland!

MARX AND HISTORY AS TRANSCENDENCE

However we choose to read Karl Marx, he clearly saw the contradiction between the means of production and modes of production as the central driving force behind the great social transformations. New means of production would burst through the constraining frames defined by the old social mode of production. A new social formation would emerge. Thus, Soviet planning dictatorship was compatible with mega-factories and mega-cooperatives, with thousands of workers, and thousands of peasants. But millions of small *samizdat*, self-made, not only kitchen publishing houses for authors, but kitchen gardens for farmers, were able to escape from the dictatorship of planning.

And then along came IT, information technology, and made industrial planning and production at the micro-level possible. The enormous pyramid controlled by the Party from the top down became a set of bigger and smaller pyramids controlled by Capital. And that is already the nucleus of a Marxist explanation of the fall of socialism and emergence of capitalism in the Soviet Union.

Any system likes to show how clever they are at solving problems and taking on challenges. What the capitalist system can produce seems to be limitless; except well-being for all. But in order to solve contradictions transcendence and transformation are needed. We have given a number of examples at the micro- and meso-levels; the macro- and mega-examples will follow. Marx was working on the big meso-transformations, and his genius found a common formula for the driving forces, covering the transition from primitive communism to slavery to feudalism to capitalism to socialism to communism: new means of production forcing a change in mode of production.

As party to the Western theory of progress he would probably have seen Russia's fall back into capitalism as temporary. Others would see more factors at play, like political structure, democracy instead of dictatorship, as a driving force in addition to the economic deep structures that served as a basis for the theory of that genius, and also for his onesidedness.

Our focus, however, is on confronting Marx with the diagram. So we put the means of production on one of the axes and the mode of production on the other. But isn't this incompatible with the principle that only that which has life also can have goals? No, we are thinking of those on top of the old mode of production, the nobility, and their conflict relation to the carriers of the new means of production, the capitalists, in search of cheap labour for their factories. That doesn't prevent us from working with abstractions as long as we know what we are talking about.

The contradiction was clear, deep, explosive. But why should the change of means of production always have that explosive effect on the modes of production, and not vice versa? Why cannot social relations change first, followed by the means of production? Thus, one million Germans reportedly want to live in the Mediterranean over the next decade or two. At the same time, they are Germans with ties to their own country. The two souls in the one breast of Goethe's compatriots evidently have two addresses: one in the Mediterranean and one in Germany. Climate, diet, exercise, lifestyle are motivating. And the European Union is creating the right conditions.

We are talking less and less about retired people and more about those who want to produce without doing their job in a building somewhere in Germany. The answer for an increasing number of occupations is IT, computers, mobile phones. Clearly means and modes were working on each other, as in the Soviet Union. A contradiction between new modes of production and old means of production was transcended with telematics and IT, as distinct from Marxist technologism.

Marx didn't have much feeling for compromise and withdrawal. A new social formation is going to be articulated fully and completely, not partly and partially. A neither/nor would be to turn history's clock back, and that's incompatible with his faith in progress. But his technologism was also prophetic. New gene technologies, for instance, are not easily stopped except, perhaps, through massive popular movements.

Marx is also well known for his work on the contradiction between two factors of production, capital and labour, nature being the third. As a power contradiction between capitalist and workers, between those who buy and those who sell labour, it is relatively easily handled. We had a look at that in 'the classless company' above. More frequent, however, is *struggle*.

A solidary capitalist class can place before the seller of labour the stark choice between accepting the price offered for his labour or starvation. Or emigration, but then capitalist solidarity and pressure on labour can also be globalised.

A solidary working class can do the same and place before the capitalist a choice between accepting the price for labour or closing the company. Or moving out, but then a working class on or below the starvation line will have more difficulties with global solidarity to bring effective pressure on capital.

We are still in the midst of this struggle, which is often decided by means of the ultimate force of the state, using the police and the army against the workers, never the other way round, and by the force of the people, who in principle can use a democratic majority to put some brakes on capitalism. The latter may lead to a social democratic negotiation economy, which is not a bad *compromise*. But it is not easy to find a stable equilibrium between the two.

The working class can use more power to abolish the capitalists as a class and put bureaucrats in their place; in other words, state capitalism. The capitalists can use their power to automate production and pay ever higher salaries for increasing labour productivity, thereby encouraging the workers to abolish themselves as a class. These are two extreme positions, replete with dictatorship/inefficiency and unemployment/starvation.

Neither/nor production, neither capital nor work, would point back to nature with hunter-gatherers and early forms of traditional agriculture. Many 'dark greens' are attracted to this, but it is difficult to regard it as anything more than a niche. Many enjoy the products produced by modern capitalism, and if one likes the ends, then abolishing the means is a problem.

But what about *positive transcendence*? Isn't it possible to abolish the distinction between workers and capitalists, or at least blunt it?

First effort: cooperatives, work and capital hand in hand, both doing both jobs as in the classless company. Conflict transformation through job transformation.

Second effort: tight, simple networks of many, small companies, small plots of land, many small factories, transportation, shops. Blunting contradictions by making them smaller.

Third effort: the workers are given or buy stocks in the company, and put the motivation of the capitalist on top of their own.

These three approaches do not exclude each other. In principle they should have a distributive effect as we can see many places where the first two play a major role. The capitalist can invest capital, and then his network could be flexible enough to catch seasonal unemployment. The problem would be mega-companies with such a large share of the market that they are badly hit by conjunctures, have to limit production and make thousands of workers redundant. It's not simple. But the future, particularly for developing countries, may well be located in this positive transcendence combining three approaches.

Let us add a third interpretation of the contradiction between capital and labour: the contradiction between capital-intensive and labour-intensive production. Labour-intensive production of shoes is known as the shoemaking craft. If many artisans are found under one roof it was referred to as a manufacture. As the investment in machinery per worker grows we get an industry, ultimately ending in automation. Industry, in other words, was a compromise.

Neither the extreme positions of artisanry, nor of automation, nor the neither/nor are acceptable. But how about transcendence? That was the Japanese model (which today has yielded to US 'efficiency'), with capital-intensive production for quantity and labour-intensive production for quality. Japan combined them in a both/and. Labour productivity was lower than in the USA, but general well-being was higher. Which is more important?

that are protracted, with a long period of violence, knowledge of the past is insufficient. Experience from mediation in macro- and mega-conflicts shows that the parties are located in a long, dark tunnel. They are apprehensive, confused and more interested in seeing some light at the end of the tunnel, in the *future-constructive*, than in an analysis of the wanderings in the labyrinth of the past-destructive. But both approaches are needed.

Dialogues about therapy proposals are always questioning, searching, in the subjunctive mode. What would it be like if? Even if the perspectives are written in the imperative – do this, do that – they are always temporary. They will change in the light of new data, values and dialogues. But they are all contributions to a culture of peace filled with concrete proposals for a better future.

The reader is now invited to a conflict tour round the world from the Pacific to the Mediterranean, with a focus on solutions and peace, but with a pedagogical jump back to eastern Greenland to learn an important lesson from history.

The conflicts under macro and mega are selected from about 50 conflicts on which TRANSCEND has been working (see www.transcend.org). Our perspectives on the conflicts are solution-oriented, so readers who want to know more about the history of the conflicts are referred to encyclopaedias and books about the countries in question. Our culture, particularly our media culture, is long on descriptions of the meta-conflicts that relate to the roots of the conflict like a metastasis to the primary tumour. There is a focus on negative attitudes = hatred, and on negative behaviour = violence, and much less focus on the contradiction roots.

Our culture is short on diagnosis of the roots of the conflicts, on prognosis, about what is happening and proposals for therapy; DPT – TRANSCEND's pillars. The pillar of the media is violence, and reporting violence is sometimes called 'objectivity'. Many journalists seem to need bombs as a wake-up call.

The first thing we do is identify the extreme positions in the conflict. In a culture like our own the number 2, and a tendency to work with two alternatives, are included in the word 'alternative'. These positions are then used to construct the basic diagram in the way the parties conceive of it themselves. Then we start looking for interesting interpretations of the other three positions, particularly of neither/nor and both/and. The reader may not believe it, but it is incredible how many conflict parties there are who get an 'a-ha' feeling when the basic figure is drawn during a dialogue with NGO grass-root members, guerrillas, presidents, of both genders, and 2 suddenly becomes 5.

How many genders? Two? At least five! Get a sheet of paper, sketch a little and you will work it out for yourself.

We are usually invited by one of the parties, or by some organisation like the UN, OSCE, etc. Usually there are few things parties in a conflict like more than the opportunity to put their case, and they usually talk more freely with an outside dialogue partner than in negotiations. The perspectives start emerging; if not, try more dialogues, using more conflict workers. Like so much creativity, the transcendence often emerges at night, to be written down in the pale light of dawn.

The basic formula for good conflict work is to escape from the tyranny of the number 2, the dichotomy with only two possibilities. But the condition for this is that there is *something* reasonable, valid, in both extreme positions, something that we can hold on to in the dialogues and build on. 'There is something good in every human being' finds another expression in the dialogue situation: 'There is something valid in every position.' Thus, the valid point in Hitler's position was his critique of the Versailles Peace Treaty of 1919. If the Allies had been able to build on that validity, we might have avoided the Second World War.

Today, we use international law and human rights as a compass to make sure we are heading in the right direction. And when this compass has a western deviation, we have to base ourselves on basic needs.

What then emerges is creative, new, unusual, soft and sometimes complicated, particularly if we combine elements from the whole peace diagonal. Ideally, the proposal should not provoke anybody, unless they have been living too long as dichotomy slaves to be able to liberate themselves. That is also the case for many independence movements. If they are fighting against a totally illegitimate, grotesque colonialism, then we are not asking for compromise or transcendence, but for liberation. And the proposal would be within the general framework of *peace by peaceful means*, which in that case means non-violent struggle. In most conflict parties there is something valid. The task is to build an acceptable and sustainable transformation on something valid, even if that 'something' is minuscule.

These perspectives will be sown like seeds in fields that are untilled, unploughed and more likely under asphalt than on top of it. Some seeds will germinate quickly; others will need watering. Some have no life force at all. And there will be counter-forces from the status quo and from hardened dichotomy slaves whose image of the world is that 'there is no alternative' (TINA, Margaret Thatcher's slogan).

These perspectives contribute to a culture of peace. A true peace culture will produce a rich flora of peace perspectives. And in a democracy we are all gardeners – nobody has a monopoly on peace.

This introduction can now be brought to an end in classic mode:

'I have bad news and good news.'

'Let us start with the bad news!'

'There is an incredible lack of creativity, of innovative skills in the politics between states and nations!'

'And the good news?'

'It is equally incredible how easy it is to learn to become more creative.'

The ten macro-level conflicts we are exploring come from different parts of the world. They are diverse, but they have features in common. To understand the seriousness of what we are going to explore we have to ask ourselves a basic question – what does it mean to live in an area ridden by deep conflict, for instance in Hawai'i, Colombia, Rwanda, Ulster, the Basque Country, Yugoslavia, Israel-Palestine?

First, there is anxiety about violence. This has five distinct aspects:

'It is political, to impose the will of the perpetrator.'

'It also hurts the non-violent, the innocent, civilians.'

'It carries in its wake panic, humiliation, terror.'

'It is unpredictable in its choice of time, space and/or victim.'

'The perpetrator will try to protect himself from retaliation.'

There are two types of perpetrators: those against the state and those for the state; terrorists and state terrorists. The five points are equally valid for both. Fear of becoming a victim works on the body, mind and spirit and reduces human beings relative to what they might have been. The same applies to the perpetrator who is producing that suffering and destruction. The trauma that consists in having traumatised others can be considerable.

The violence between perpetrator and victim is only a small part of the total violence. We will be treated to the conventional military headquarters communiqué: numbers killed, numbers wounded, material destruction, as misleading and false as the image the media give of the economic (read: stock exchange) reality. Those who are deprived are rarely mentioned: family, friends, neighbours, colleagues. On average maybe ten for every person killed; ten people suffering his/her suffering and carrying it into the future; ten feeling hatred building up; ten calling for revenge and/or giving in to despair, apathy. The act of violence is reborn and reincarnated on a daily basis.

Then there are those who have been neither killed nor visibly wounded: the raped, the externally or internally displaced, the refugees.

They can all build their lives around their hatred. But this will never be a really rich and creative life. Every day we can hear, at the micro- and meso-levels, stories of violence from people forever marked by conflict and violence. They have become *offended*, and have built their lives around the injustice they feel they have suffered. They become dark, sombre persons who radiate nothing, like black holes in the social universe, rather than a source of light that can shine within them, and for others.

But the history of violence is also the history of a nature that is bombed, mined, raped, humiliated and has become a giant waste tip of military debris, some of it toxic.

A society structured for violence becomes a caricature of itself, whether the violence comes from the top of a steep power pyramid or from small guerrilla cells; as state terrorism from above or terrorism from below. The culture becomes a storehouse of deep wounds, way into the collective memory and soul of that people, wounds that are used to misunderstand everything and everybody rather than to search for new approaches.

In short: violence creates humans incapable of reconciliation and reunion, more fit for retaliation.

Then there is the conflict itself, the incompatibility, the goals blocking each other. What this means is above all that political life is paralysed. The conflict is like a tumour sucking energy from everywhere in the social organism, away from distribution of economic resources, for instance. In social life the conflict drives a wedge between the parties, and at the personal level the conflict takes the form of hatred gnawing at people's hearts. Culturally, the victims are dreaming of revenge and revanche, and the perpetrators are dreaming of more victories, always with themselves as the victors.

Social and personal generosity is shrinking to a very narrow spectrum of self-righteousness and images of the maliciousness of the other side, with no empathy and compassion. At the same time they are waiting in hope and awe for release through new violence.

Time is standing still. Societies are not developing. Nor are human beings, unless we conceive of preparation for violence and hatred and heroism, with a risk of killing and being killed, and destruction, as development. Our societies become caricatures of themselves, even if there is something positive to say about the cohesion in the two camps. Human beings also become caricatures, like shadows in the waiting room of history. The conflict locks humans, groups and the whole of society into that waiting room, and leaves them to the sado-masochists. The train on the short-distance track has been stationed there, exposed to the elements. On the long-distance tracks ever more elegant express trains are speeding past. They do not stop, the passengers are pointing to the waiting room: there they are, those poor people, we really should pity them. And those in the waiting room are desperately hoping for somebody to come from the outside, to incapacitate the sado-masochists, to open the doors, to get the train started again. Their own creativity is something they lost a long time ago.

The three characteristics so important in this book, empathy and creativity to find solutions, and non-violence to practise them, have been killed or been 'birth controlled' away, leaving the ground for the preparation of the cruelty of violence itself. What is lost is not only the suffering that comes from violence, but equally the absence of the joy of full development, both personally and socially.

Hence conflicts must be transformed so that the parties can live creatively and non-violently and the violence avoided. The parties have to break down the polarisation within themselves and between them because it makes empathy, dialogue and creativity as impossible as deep understanding and dialogue with ebola, HIV, cholera or bubonic plague, with scorpions. Peace building = depolarisation + humanisation is indispensable.

Should violence take place, then reconciliation is needed in order to start from the beginning again. Difficult, but that in itself is no excuse for suffering due to a lacking ability, or will, to find a real solution.

ECUADOR–PERU: BI-NATIONAL ZONE, NATURAL PARK

- *Very creative*, the former Ecuadorean president said when he heard the proposal to solve the border conflict in a zone of

500 km² which had led to three wars between Ecuador and Peru, not by drawing any border at all, but by turning it into a 'bi-national zone, with a natural park'. Nobody has proposed that so far!

- But, he said, *too creative*. It will take at least 30 years just to get used to the idea, and then at least another 30 years to implement it. However, permit me one question: how did you arrive at that idea?

I could, of course, have answered that it was not because I knew history and that I knew my Latin America, but above all because I had a certain diagram firmly imprinted on my brain so that my advice was quite predictable. They had practised postponement, withdrawal, for 54 years, combined with endless negotiations. They had also tried total military victory. Compromise had been attempted by drawing a new border dividing the territory. The only possibility left was transcendence, and the simplest both/and was the bi-national zone. But my answer was somewhat more detailed:

- I have a little method, and that is to listen to what has not been said, listen to the inaudible. Neither you nor your colleague has said anything about why one has to draw a border, probably because you think it is too obvious. You are probably both of the opinion that every square metre on this our earth belongs to one and only one country. And it is like that, almost 100 per cent. The method consists in identifying axioms of faith which are not to be discussed, not even to be formulated, and then start touching them, tinkering with them, shaking them, inserting the word 'not', negating them so that everything becomes more flexible. As a general rule this will lead us to something that can be changed. But, as you pointed out yourself, it can easily become too creative, precisely because it touches articles of faith.

We parted as friends after a better dinner, without any appointment.

But this became the basis of the peace treaty between Ecuador and Peru three years later, in autumn 1998, after Ecuador had proposed a 'bi-national zone, with a natural park'. The prediction by the ex-president had been proved false. No 30 + 30 = 60 years were needed, but a mere three years. The parties had committed themselves to arrive at an agreement in 1998, and that became a transcendence according to the TRANSCEND formula. Something as simple as this took 57 years after the first war in 1941. And after that there were three more wars, and an effort to draw a boundary by using a watershed which became too complicated, and a river which appeared and disappeared, according to temperature and rainfall. And a border was only a compromise anyway.

The interpretation of 'both/and' in a border conflict as a 'both/and zone', or 'bi-national zone', is rather simple. Neither/nor, giving the zone to the UN for instance, is also simple, but was unacceptable. That simplicity made it easy even for people well trained in history, international law and possible precedents (drawing conclusions from similar cases) to accept a proposal, even within the framework of the type of verbal warfare referred to as 'negotiations', with its many subterfuges, overt and covert. Of course, it was also very useful that the zone was unpopulated and poor in resources.

Two other factors certainly also played a role.

So much *time* had had elapsed since 1941 that they had tried both legal and, when that did not work, military solutions. Their efforts were based on a very limited repertoire of solutions: one of them wins; the case is dismissed; or a cease-fire with the border along the line of cease-fire. The obsession with drawing a border was blocking transcendence. And in addition they were not even able to draw a border.

For that reason the *point in time* was just right. The whole thing had become a scandal. They were tired of the whole conflict. The key was not buried in historical legitimation from the past, but in a little bit of creativity about the future. And not in a good chemistry between them, but within them.

Successful conflict transformation requires creativity, but is very inexpensive. The dialogue with the President of Ecuador cost $125 for a stopover in Quito and a night in a hotel – far less than what governments typically spend on diplomacy. By comparison, the usual approach of military intervention after violence breaks out costs billions of dollars. Peaceful conflict transformation before a war, peaceful pre-emption, can save very many lives and allow society to move on.

EAST GREENLAND: NORWAY/DENMARK 'FORGOT' THE INUITS

Here is the case, a little simplified, in the World Court held in The Hague in 1933 between Norway and Denmark over east Greenland, with its Inuit population:

Norway: The land is ours. We discovered it, we were the first to lay
eyes on it. We came, we saw, we conquered – *veni, vidi,
vici*. The land belongs to he who discovers it.

Denmark: It is true that Norwegians arrived first; the Norwegians
are great travellers. We came later. We baptised them,
alphabetised them, gave them a written language, a bible,
gave them law and justice, courts and punishment, taught
them new techniques to get food and housing. In short, we
civilised them. The land belongs to he who develops it.

Here we get not only the positions, but also the justification, the
legitimation, clearly expressed. The Court's decision was unanimously
in favour of Denmark for having shown *animus occupandi*, the spirit of
the possessor, with responsibility, care, development. The Norwegians
arrived first but left after their 'discovery'.

Conflict Worker: Well, what do the participants have to say?

Eager, but somewhat naïve participant:

A both/and solution as for Ecuador–Peru! Norway
and Denmark own and develop the land together.
They can also bring in other Nordic countries,
Iceland perhaps, which actually is green, in order
to help Greenland, which actually consists mostly
of ice.

Conflict Worker: I am sorry, but you have fallen into the trap prepared
for you by presenting this example immediately
after Ecuador–Peru. Always remember that the first
thing you do in a conflict analysis, after you have
mapped the parties, goals and contradictions, is to
divide the goals into the legitimate and illegitimate.
But you can of course rightly ask, how do we know
whether a goal is legitimate or illegitimate?

Here is a rule of thumb: if the realisation of a goal is against human
basic needs/basic rights, then it is illegitimate. Basic needs mean
survival with physical well-being – that is, biologically given needs
reasonably satisfied, living a life in freedom, with identity and
meaning. Human rights mirror this, not perfectly, but as a good
approximation. For that reason use basic needs as your guide.

The problem here is the needs of the Inuits, and their fundamental
right to *freedom*, meaning independence/sovereignty, and to *identity/*

meaning as defined by their own culture, even if the other two basic needs are well taken care of by Denmark. A right is objective, independent of the subjective consciousness about it. These rights exist even if the Inuits do not demand them.

We can still use the diagram, but we have to turn the axes round. The goal is now 'not belonging to Norway', and 'not belonging to Denmark', and certainly not 'belonging to both Norway and Denmark', which would be tantamount to double colonialism. It reminds me of the situation in Tahiti (Polynésie 'française') on 15 June 1989. There were elections to the Parliament of the European Community. The elections were boycotted by the Polynesians, who said that colonialism by twelve countries (the number of EC members at the time) was no better than colonialism by France alone. The right-wing Front National led by Jean-Marie Le Pen carried the day among the small white minority.

There are two obvious interpretations of 'neither Norway, nor Denmark':

(1) The Inuits own East Greenland (or exercise a very high level of autonomy);
(2) East Greenland is administered by the League of Nations.

Both are clear negative transcendences of the original conflict. The case had been launched as Norway against Denmark; the Inuits and the League of Nations had not been considered.

The poverty of due process of law is illustrated by this example. It's a question of adjudication between *two* parties. A neither/nor opinion referring to the right of self-determination, well known in 1933 if only for white nations, might have had as a consequence that the judge had been declared mentally ill. Compromise and transcendence are beyond that legal paradigm. And dismissal of the case means capitulation of the court as a mechanism of conflict resolution.

A possible transformation could build on a combination of everything that has been mentioned, except the extreme positions. The goal is independence for the Inuits. But the means could have included an element of Norwegian/Danish cooperation within the framework of the League of Nations, with Norway as expert in fisheries and Denmark in agriculture. In other words, the entire main diagonal again: the peace diagonal.

HAWAI'I: SOVEREIGNTY AS A PROCESS

Hawai'ian citizen of Hawai'i: Hawai'i, the whole archipelago, all eight islands, belongs to us. White settlers colonised us from the first contact in 1778. Businessmen and US marines committed the first military coup in the Pacific against the Hawai'ian monarchy in 1893. They annexed Hawai'i in 1898 and Hawai'i became the fiftieth US state in 1959. All of this was illegitimate, coming from the outside and from above, at the expense of the Hawai'ians. Had more than half the population been Hawai'ian, Hawai'i would have been decolonised after 1945. But they killed us in so many different ways, and substituted white people and yellow people until they comprised the majority in a plebiscite. They call that democracy.

They bought our land and deprived many of us of our livelihood. They gave us diseases to which we had no immunity and referred to that as Acts of God. The missionaries took children away from their parents and sent them to the USA to teach them English, Christianity and baseball so that they could become good Americans. They took our culture, they made us homeless. We became the easy prey of alcohol, drugs, theft, prison, accidents, and we lived short, unhappy lives. 'Post-Traumatic Stress Disorder', PTSD, is what they call it.

There were 800,000 of us when we were 'discovered', as they call it. In the end there were only 8,000 full-blood Hawai'ians left. They talk a lot about genocide, these people. We know what that means. Today about 20 per cent of the population can call themselves Hawai'ian; the whites make up about 25 per cent. The rest are mainly east Asians brought in as cruelly exploited agricultural workers; they used them to cultivate *our* land, for *them*. The settlers used the land for plantations, only to be out-competed by Mexico. The military bases earned us a Japanese attack. Their tourism falsifies our culture. We got rich, but the land is ours. We want it back and we shall treat those who live there better than they treated us.

White citizen of Hawai'i: Well, well, well. If we hadn't come, you would still have been climbing your coconut palm trees. OK, some of us were a little bit too enthusiastic. But our intentions were good. And all of this has been to your benefit. You can now enjoy it, fully, provided you obey the laws and work hard, like we do.

Conflict Worker: Classic. Historically, Hawai'i belongs to the Hawai'ians; democratically, it belongs to the majority who are not Hawai'ian but have come to stay. The future then reproduces the present, the status quo, with the indigenous population as second-class citizens in their own country.

But then came November 1993 with President Clinton's 'apology to indigenous Hawai'ians on behalf of the USA for having committed a coup against the kingdom of Hawai'i' (Public Law 103–150). Good. The Hawai'ians straightened their backs. But the danger is that this will be followed by the US 'nation within a nation', well known from the reservations established for American Indians, with South African apartheid as a nightmare. An apology, land restored to some Hawai'ians and compensation are not enough. And the immigrants cannot simply be thrown out – many of them have lived there for generations.

Negative transcendence, giving the archipelago to others, is meaningless. What is left is compromise and positive transcendence.

Divide the archipelago into two? A 'state within the state'? That's not impossible. But they live among each other, and everybody wants access to the whole paradise. By what right should Hawai'ians, a 'minority' according to that shameful democratic theory, live by the grace of the majority in part of their own country? They all have to own it together, but with more power to the Hawai'ians than there is today.

Two problems have to be solved: the relationship to continental USA, and the relationship between Hawai'ians and the others inside Hawai'i.

If the 1893 coup and the annexation in 1898 were illegal, then autonomy in foreign–security–finance policies is a solution. An interesting model is Hong Kong relative to China, which would imply neither classical independence nor federation, but some kind of confederation with the USA, and with the rest of Polynesia, with Rapa Nui (Easter Island), Tahiti, Samoa, Aotearoa (New Zealand). A moderate solution, with advantages for all. A legislative assembly with two chambers, one democratic for all citizens, one historical for Hawai'ians, is also a possibility, with self-determination and a veto over everything that concerns Hawai'ian culture. They can also reconquer much of Hawai'i as an archipelago of 'sacred places' and endow it with a tight calendar of 'sacred times', in memory of the traumas and triumphs of the past. Deep respect for Hawai'ian culture would be the basic rule, with both Hawai'ian and English as administrative languages.

That non-Hawai'ians have to accept such fundamental aspects of the cultural Hawai'i as respect for nature and for other nations is self-evident. Most already do. A Hawai'i of that kind could also combine a strong financial economy with a strongly basic needs-oriented and self-reliant productive economy. They could build on the links to the entire Pacific hemisphere. And they could build security on good relations with all, disband the army and use the many military bases for UN troops.

COLOMBIA: BUILD A SOCIETY, NOT ONLY A STATE

Colombian, from the bottom 70 per cent socially, coloured: Our work is insufficient to provide for our basic needs, which are eroded on a daily basis. On the land, with or without a little plot, in the towns, with or without a miserable job, life is short, filled with misery, disease, violence. All we want is a sustainable life lived in dignity and safety. If the only way of protecting my family passes through cultivating or selling drugs in order to meet the enormous demand from the *gringos* in the USA, or by pilfering a little from the rich who have more than enough, or through a violent revolution, then we will do one, two or all three.

Colombian, from the top 30 per cent socially, white: Our life is threatened by the violence all around us, and that menace is increasing every day. Our country has become a centre for the production and distribution of drugs. Theft, including hostage-taking for ransom, is the order of the day. Even murder takes place with close to 100 per cent impunity. The police and the courts have ceased to function. If the road to security passes through violence, whether military or paramilitary, with the assistance of the USA and in the worst case with direct military invasion from the USA and some allies, then we are in favour of that.

Conflict Worker: These are among the things to be transcended. Colombia is a grotesquely divided society with sharp class and race contradictions, certainly not a homogeneous Nordic country with a workers–peasants–fishermen alliance building a welfare state by taxing the rich and redistributing wealth to the poor. Let us hear the voices of six Colombia experts, each with their own diagnosis:

A: An extreme case of *poderes fácticos* (*latifundistas, militares, cleros*) in power, highly hierarchical and exploitative. If you belong to a trade union, the landowner will throw you out, the military will kill you and the clergy will send your soul to hell. The result is violence from below (guerrillas, FARC/ELN) and counter-violence from above (*para-militares*), in shifting civil war fronts.

B: A two-party system carrying nineteenth-century agendas, incapable of absorbing into public space and political debate social democracy, green-ism, communism (guerrillas) and fascism (*para-militares*).

C: After the murder of the trade union leader Gaitán on 9 April 1948 a civil war (*la violencia*) has been raging, killing opposition voters with impunity.

D: An extreme case of drug trafficking, with Colombia as supplier, profits to key power-holders and distribution along very violent economic cycles.

E: Public space has degenerated into an anarchic battlefield, with corruption, between the groups described in A–D. An extreme case of anomie, dissolution of social norms–values–culture regulating public space behaviour, with impunity for murder. And an extreme case of *atomie*, dissolution of the social fabric, structure, of public space, with fragmentation and atomisation. These conditions produce violence, corruption, drug chains with us as producers and distributors and the consumers in the USA, and sect formation with the violent groups as sects where people find leadership and social fabric. In short, a total social crisis. This is no longer a viable society.

F: On top of this the risk of a US invasion is building, using D as a pretext to stop A, unless the Colombian government can do the job for them, and only if other Latin American countries participate. The USA does not want to act unilaterally.

Conflict Worker: Experts, this was diagnosis. Do you have any therapies?

A: The pact paradigm between governments and guerrillas assumes that cohesive cultures will honour a promise, and cohesive structures are binding on others. Under anomie and atomie this is not the case. In addition there is the temptation to see a pact as an end, not as a means. General point: let us have more facts and fewer pacts. We need less, not more, faith in pacts.

B: The multi-party political paradigm can also be counteracted by making elections more ritualistic, and parliament less relevant.

C: The legal paradigm with more state, more police and more punishment presupposes cohesive structures and cultures in public space, and they simply do not exist.

D: The war-on-drugs paradigm is meaningful only if the whole economic cycle, with the root causes of demand, as well as the anomie and atomie in consumer countries like the USA, are effectively confronted, as well as such factors as chemicals and air transport. One problem is how to find economic substitutes to make peace profitable. Certification by producer countries of US efforts to remove US causes of drug demand?

E: The institutional paradigm intended to provide public space with efficiently and honestly operating institutions is counteracted by anomie and atomie, and by highly dubious police and military.

F: *The Plan Colombia* paradigm, leaving the task increasingly to the USA and OAS, can create long-lasting dependency and colonisation.

Conflict Worker: Two conclusions from this round-table debate: you don't yourselves believe in the proposals that follow from the factor you highlighted. And you repeatedly mention two underlying factors, *atomie* and *anomie*. The basic problem is how to build a society. But to do that you need hard work:

- *Against anomie*: (re)creating a sense of compelling norms and values; a very challenging task for the Church and particularly for younger priests, and for school and family as the key agents of socialisation in society. It is a question of (re)creating the traffic rules in public space, starting with norms like 'Thou shalt not kill' and 'Thou shalt not steal', and with values of solidarity with the poor, against the egoistic cost-benefit analysis and materialist individualism of economism. Moral, social and world leadership are badly needed.
- *Against atomie*: (re)creating social fabric in public space, weaving a tight web of criss-crossing NGOs of many types, with multiple memberships, not forgetting kinship, friends, work and worship groups, serving as conduits for norms of solidarity.

Then:

(1) Increase the capacity for handling conflicts at all social levels, expanding conflict repertoires, using weekly church, school and TV courses for years to combat conflict illiteracy.

(2) Empower women and young people as conflict/peace workers, training them as mediators.

(3) Introduce peace and conflict education in schools, making available texts with 50–100 stories of successful non-violent and creative conflict handling as reference points throughout life.

(4) Introduce peace journalism in the media, focusing more on root conflicts and possible outcomes and processes, and less on the violent meta-conflict and who is winning; focusing more on people and less on elites.

(5) Build disarmed peace zones based on confederations of municipalities and the points mentioned above, then upgrade the zones by adding more points, and introduce international protection of the zones.

(6) For international peacekeeping, with neighbouring countries helping, use Sun Tzu, not Clausewitz, as the doctrine. Use police methods, non-violence and mediation. Let many of the peacekeepers be women. Reject any US invasion.

(7) *Truth and reconciliation* commissions along South African rather than Central American lines, using the courts, Church, psychology, TV.

(8) Conduct business (like coffee) along modern lines with much higher returns for the workers/producers, cutting out the middlemen.

(9) Establish subsistence economies with micro-credits, adequate technology, cooperatives, etc. alongside the growth economy.

(10) Attack pathologies in Colombian culture, such as machismo and the cult of violence head-on, as part of the anti-anomie struggle.

(11) Create higher levels of internal security by retraining police and military for all the tasks mentioned above.

(12) Use human rights, including economic, social and cultural rights, as moral guidelines for a vibrant democracy.

All of this has to be done in parallel/synchronically, not sequentially, in order to create a society where this deep class conflict can be transcended.

RWANDA/THE GREAT LAKES: A BI-OCEANIC CONFEDERATION

There are many factors behind the genocide in 1994. Much of it goes beyond Rwanda. The labels 'Tutsi'/'Hutu', with 'moderate Hutu', point to race, class and people afraid of losing power and profit. Some roots are located in German colonialism and *Rassenkunde* (race 'science'), favouring the Tutsis over the Hutus and both over the 'pygmies', being taller. The Belgian successors to the German colonialists after the First World War favoured the Hutu majority, 'numbers over centimetres', because democracy was 'in'. After colonialism came economic neo-colonialism, and the West was gambling on the Hutus, afraid of losing Zaire/Congo.

Another aspect of the conflict is the projection of the Anglo-French European tribal feud over linguistic, cultural and economic influence in Africa. Uganda/Tutsi/Kabila Anglophiles are pitted against Hutu/Mobutu Francophiles, with the Western media traditionally dominated by the French as 'area specialists'. But disasters tend to favour the spread of English as most disasters are managed by the UN in English. French and Roman Law are losing ground it seems, and English/Common Law is pushing westward, with consequences for property law.

A third aspect is the role played by development aid, and particularly Swiss aid. Development agencies want successes and tend to play on dominant groups in society, thereby reinforcing class relations, which may be explosive. The underprivileged see no alternative to migration and then invasion; the overprivileged see no alternative to pre-emptive violence against those lower down. The result: emigration, genocide and invasion.

If the conditions producing genocide are located in the structure of Rwandan society and in a culture of violence, they have to be changed. But tribunals locate the conditions in evil actors, and remove them by execution or imprisonment. The same conditions will produce the same result, only with different personnel.

If we look at this as a conflict between the two groups, then the five outcomes are clear, but not very encouraging:

(1) All power to the Hutus – which is what they had.
(2) All power to the Tutsis with moderate Hutus – which is what they now have.
(3) Leave it all to international or African administration.
(4) Compromise, elections, oscillating between (1) and (2).
(5) Encourage the emergence of a general Rwandan personality.

The last two look good on paper. But (5) is a utopia and (4) implies a party system building on national identities that could freeze the situation. (1) and (2) privilege one group over the other. We are left with some kind of negative transcendence.

Conflict worker: One point of departure might be to question the availability of any lasting outcome within the narrow confines of Rwanda. Too much hatred per square kilometre?

Thus, a married couple might find solutions to their problems outside the narrow confines of their apartment (note 'apart'). And the solution to Rwanda might be located outside Rwanda.

One possible approach might be a *bi-oceanic confederation* from the Indian to the Atlantic Oceans, including Uganda and Tanzania, Rwanda and Burundi, the two Congos, and maybe other countries. That confederation could trade East–West, with West–South Asia and Central–South America, as much as North–South. There would be open borders for people and ideas, goods and services, not confining people with a tradition of enmity to a very limited territory. Japan, with extensive programmes for Africa, could contribute with East–West rail/road infrastructure and services. New energies could be tapped, exploiting the bi-oceanic opportunities, as the Republic of South Africa does skilfully.

It would also be useful if Germany, Belgium, France and Switzerland, the USA and not only the UN could acknowledge their responsibility for the genocide, contributing to reconciliation by taking some of that colossal burden off local shoulders. The burden is too great for such a small country. Better bring in others, identify causes, run massive programmes in the culture of peace, create a new geopolitical reality, reconcile, mobilising all forces for peace. A new future is important, but the past also has to be processed. A tribunal is incapable of doing all that.

ULSTER: FUNCTIONAL INDEPENDENCE

Let us start with three statements and three clear goals, reproduced with some liberty from a hearing outside Dublin, in August 1997:

Protestant, Northern Ireland: I love England. I love rationality, clear analysis, not hot, clammy, tear-stained words, songs, music. I love English diversity, the debate, the tension. I detest the monotony of the Roman Church where faith, thought and speech are all the same. If they should get into power, the result would be dictatorship, the end of rationality, diversity. I would never place my children in their schools. And: they use all kinds of methods to obtain their goals. They are dangerous. For that reason we need arms to protect ourselves.

Catholic, Northern Ireland: I love Ireland. I love people who are not afraid of giving expression to their feelings in poetry, music, songs, who do not have fish blood in their veins, refer to their coldness as 'rationality' and to minuscule differences among them as 'diversity'. I do not want to have my children in their schools. They have power, and behind them is English colonialism. They have their paramilitary, they have 93 per cent of the police, they have deployed the British Army in our country. They are dangerous. For that reason we need weapons to protect ourselves.

Moderate, 'Ulsterite': I love Ulster. Protestant or Catholic, this is our land. The fundamentalists with their killings make up only a small percentage of the population, like mechanics and bartenders, building and mixing bombs, sadistic human beings who punish those who no longer want to join in their madness with kneecapping. I was one of them myself, it doesn't matter on which side. Now I know that non-violence is not only a way, but the only way. Everybody born here has an equal right to live here. Let us come together to build a new, ever more independent, Ulster, along with the Welsh and the Scots.

A standard mistake made by the media is to reduce the conflict formation (parties, goals, contradictions) to the conflict arena where there is hatred and violence – along Belfast's Shankhill Road (Protestant) and Falls Road (Catholic). The parties are reduced to 2, a simple number with which to work. And the contradictions are reduced to religion. Class disappears, of course. They are afraid of losing their religious identity in an ocean of Protestant majorities in Ulster and the United Kingdom, and in a Catholic majority in a United Ireland. London's goal and role are rendered invisible, but not the well-known goals of the two groups: the United Kingdom of Great Britain and Northern Ireland for the Protestants (*Unionists*), and a United Irish Republic of 26 counties in the south and six in the north, $26 + 6 = 1$, for the Catholics (*Republicans*). In this way the traditional media manage to draw a veil over possible solutions.

For *London* Ireland was the first colony, and Northern Ireland is likely to become the last. The loss will be traumatic to some. Then comes *Dublin* where the old dream of a united Ireland now is latent. Then there is the *Irish diaspora in the USA*; that's also important because the USA is important. And then a major conflict party is made invisible, the *moderate majority*, perhaps 85 per cent in Ulster, the carriers of a third, transcending possibility, but uninteresting for incompetent journalists getting their stories from bombs and violence.

The two extreme sectarian positions are increasingly irrelevant. People are tired of violence. They are searching for combinations along the peace diagonal and for reduction of violence as the result of open, honest agreements, not secret deals behind closed doors.

This proposal by TRANSCEND combined points on the peace diagonal and was presented at the Glencree Centre near Dublin in August 1997, and in a committee room in the House of Commons in March 1998, as guiding principles for a peaceful outcome:

(1) A transitional Anglo-Irish condominium is substituted for the present status for Northern Ireland, with a view to a very high level of autonomy/independence for Ulster after X years. Neither 'UK', nor 'Northern Ireland', convey autonomy.

(2) The six counties would constitute Ulster as an entity – actually six of the nine counties in Ulster with the remaining three being in the Republic of Ireland – with no internal borders, and could for the period of transition be considered a territory of both England and Ireland. Any resident could opt for a British or an Irish passport. Voting and some other rights in Britain or Ireland would go with the passport; not excluding voting and other rights in Ulster.

(3) Ultimately, the right of Ulsterites to self-rule has to be recognised. The definition of an 'Ulsterite' could be one who defines him/herself as an Ulsterite, not tied to blood quantum, cultural tradition or duration of residence. Respect for Ulster, its inhabitants, and a sense of homeland, would be more basic.

(4) A parliament, Stormont, already exists for the Ulster entity, with a government accountable to the parliament; non-sectarian parties have gradually to be in command.

(5) Two assemblies might be elected for and by the Protestant and the Catholic communities, with veto rights in matters relating to their patrimony, and local police/courts.

(6) There might be a Governing Council with five members, one representative from London, one from Dublin, one from the Protestant community, one from the Catholic community and one from the Ulster Parliament, to guide a process towards ever-increasing autonomy, and to mediate among the communities.

(7) Ulster would then gradually attain international identity:

   (a) An Ulster passport would be recognised, first within the British Isles and the European Union, then globally, in addition to the British or Irish (EU) passports. Thus, every Ulsterite is entitled to two passports, but may choose only one.

   (b) British pounds and Irish euros would be welcomed anywhere.

   (c) The euro might have a local version with the same value (an ulster?). To stimulate local economies a discount for deals in ulsters might be considered. Investment in high-tech industries and services would be encouraged.

   (d) The budget for Ulster would be based on additional sources of revenue (duties, VAT) as for an EU country, with an EU subsidy; monitoring the distribution among the communities.

   (e) Special treaties would handle relations with London and Dublin, to be implemented by the Governing Council, with review clauses guaranteeing revision every Y years (Y = X = 25?).

   (f) The entity would be demilitarised and renounce the right to have a separate army. Its security would be guaranteed jointly by Britain and Ireland together, in cooperation with the OSCE and the UN.

   (g) The British Army would be withdrawn, the police force made truly non-sectarian and the IRA/UDF encouraged to disarm bilaterally.

   (h) The entity would have observer status in the European Union, other European organisations and the UN.

   (i) Massive aid from the European Union, other European organisations and the UN could be tuned to a peaceful progress.

   (j) Independence should not be excluded, provided there is a clear majority in both communities.

   (k) Some redrawing of the borders should not be excluded, using a voting process at the municipal level similar to the Danish–German model for Schleswig-Holstein 1920.

In other words, the transcendence is negative: neither London, nor Dublin. Hard work is needed.

And then some guiding principles for a peace process:

(1) Giving priority to conflict resolution may make violence dwindle away, giving priority to arms/violence control may encourage it. In addition, a conflict left unresolved may encourage violence. There are no absolute truths in conflict theory and practice, but this is probably a better rule of thumb than most. To give first priority to violence control ('decommissioning') plays into the court of violent parties which can break any agreement with one bomb, and policing is very expensive. Moreover, why should they give up their means of violence when no conflict resolution is in sight? The parties also worry about their own security. But the best approach is to find exits from a conflict that has become stuck, acceptable to all parties and reasonably sustainable, and the remaining proponents of violence will probably be very few and far between, and easily controlled by soft methods. Give them the impression that violence control is the first priority and fronts will harden, and not only among the very few who engage in violence for its own sake.

(2) Let a thousand dialogues blossom. That conflict resolution affecting millions in a most basic way is too important to leave to a handful of politicians/diplomats/statesman is a truism in a democracy, overcoming a remnant of feudal periods in our history. Ultimately, the people, the ultimate sovereign in democracies, must be given a chance in a referendum. But voting does not tap people's creativity. Organise dialogues, not only debates, everywhere, in small groups, take notes, let ideas flow in a Gross National Idea Pool (GNIP), and feed that into the decision-making processes to the benefit of all.

(3) Give more space in the process to the moderate majority and less to declared Republicans and Unionists. The moderates carry less negative baggage from the past into the future.

(4) The Orange Order marches will have to come to an end or be balanced by 'Green Order' marches. Catholics have to learn to react non-violently and not be so easily provoked.

(5) There is a need for healing, for reconciliation, for closure. The following may be useful perspectives:

(a) Encounter groups, high or low in society, publicly visible or not, where parties that have committed violence against each other meet, is one way. They would share experiences and emotions, concerns and fears. There might be elements of restitution and apologies/forgiveness. But above all such groups could very profitably do the following:

- Joint reconstruction: the parties, together, repairing some material damage rather than leaving it all to construction firms (they may also be needed); helping to heal wounds, rehabilitating the physically and spiritually wounded rather than leaving it all to professionals (also needed).
- Joint resolution: the parties, together, working out the details of conflict resolution in their area.
- Joint sorrow: the parties, together, locally or everywhere, setting aside time to mark the tragedy of what happened, as an hour or a day of reflection, and also on what could have been done and what needs still to be done to prevent violence from recurring.

(b) Personal testimonies. The victims, including the bereaved, are numerous; their stories should not be forgotten. Their testimonies should be collected and made available, also to deter future generations from doing the same.

(c) A Truth and Reconciliation Commission, following the South African model.

EUSKADI: FUNCTIONAL INDEPENDENCE

As mentioned, journalists and politicians very often make the mistake of seeing only two parties in the conflict arena, the place where the ETA bombs find their targets and Madrid reacts. The contradiction between ETA and Madrid, between the goals of *independence* and of *status quo with small changes for País Vasco*, the land of the Basques, is real. But much is omitted: the French Basques, Paris, the Spanish in the Spanish País Vasco, the French in the French Pays Basque, and the many in both places who, when asked, say 'Soy Vasca y soy española' ('I'm a Basque and I'm Spanish'). So we have eight parties, and a more complex and more complete picture of the situation.

The old Basque goal is four *provincias* (in Spain) + 3 *provinces* (in France) = 1, the United Basque Country, *Euskadi*. But Paris has enjoyed a success of sorts with a Jacobin, centrally directed France, presumably without national fault lines, ever since the French Revolution. Franco tried it between 1936 and 1975, but with much less success. Extreme positions dominate the conflict, and positions beyond complete independence on the one hand, and País Vasco as one of Spain's 17 'autonomies' on the other, are very infrequent. Thus the violence continues. ETA kills with bombs. The democratic Madrid under Felipe Gonzáles and the socialists, with the secret GAL, killed far more than Franco did in the same number of years at the end of the dictatorship. Cease-fires are a part of the picture. But without a culture of peace with a dense web of visions presented in public space they will be no more than intervals between the resort to violence, perhaps even used to prepare for violent action the better. Spanish deep culture, with bullfighting as its metaphor, where a dark counterpart is vanquished by technical skill, is also blocking. The Basques are to some extent the most Spanish of Spaniards. There is little space for withdrawal, compromise or transcendence. For the time being they are engaged in parallel bullfighting. Without an injection of creativity this will go on for generations, even centuries.

A key to transcendence, and through that to conflict transformation, would be to look at the Basques as Basques *and* as Spanish or French:

(1) The right of the Basques to self-determination is recognised. The definition of 'Basque' could by self-definition be as a Basque, tied less to blood or linguistic ability than to cultural identification, and a sense of homeland.

(2) The three *provincias* and four *provinces* are defined as a Basque *entity*, *Euskadi*, with no internal border, in the EU, while also remaining parts of Spain and France.

(3) Euskadi would be trilingual, with Euskara as the official language; Spanish and French as administrative languages.

(4) The present governing organs at the level of the *autonomía* and the *département* (Basque) would continue.

(5) A Parliament (*fors*) would be elected for the Euskadi entity, with a government answerable to the assembly.

(6) There should be assemblies for the Spaniards and the French living in Euskadi, with veto rights in matters relating to their patrimony, possibly also local courts and local policing.

(7) The Euskadi entity could gradually attain more international personality, through:

    (a) A passport that could be recognised within France/Spain, the European Union, the world. Any citizen would as before be entitled to a French or Spanish (EU) passport. One possibility would be to have one passport with The European Union, Spain *or* France *and* Euskadi written on it.

(b) As with the passport, so with voting: any citizen could have one vote in Euskadi and one in Spain or France.

(c) The euro might have an Euskadi version with the same value (an euskadi?). To stimulate the local economy a discount for deals in euskadis might be considered.

(d) The budget for Euskadi would be based on the joint budget for the *autonomía* and the *département*, with additional sources of revenue (duties, VAT) as for any EU country, and the same pattern of expenditure.

(e) Special treaties would handle relations with Paris and Madrid, with review clauses/revision every N years (N = 25?); or when the inexhaustible right to self-determination is exercised.

(f) Euskadi would be demilitarised, renouncing the right to have a separate army. External security would be guaranteed by Spain and France, in cooperation with OSCE and the UN.

(g) Euskadi would have observer status in the EU, other European organisations and the UN.

(h) Euskadi develops its own foreign policy over time.

(i) Dual citizenship, *de facto* and *de jure*, might be considered.

(j) Independence, federation, confederation, association, etc. are all options implied in the right of self-determination.

(k) Some redrawing of borders might be considered, using voting at the local level, as in the Danish–German 1920 model.

(8) The process would at any time keep the outcome open.

(9) A reconciliation process has to be initiated.

(10) The process calls for both elite and people participation.

There is a model in the Pyrenees: *Andorra*. Madrid and Paris need to learn that the world will not collapse if a Franco-Spanish condominium leads to independence. And ETA should learn how much more they can achieve without violence.

YUGOSLAVIA: EQUAL RIGHT TO SELF-DETERMINATION

Conflict Worker: What is it you really want? What are the goals?

Slovene: We are a nation, with the same right as any other nation to have our own state through self-determination for the first time. We want to be ruled neither from Vienna nor from Belgrade, but from Ljubljana and, in a broader European context, from Brussels. Our small minorities are safe in a democracy with human rights.

Croat: We are a nation, with the same right as any other nation to have our own state through self-determination. We want to be ruled neither from Vienna nor from Belgrade, but from Zagreb and, in a broader European context, from Brussels. Our minorities can feel safe in a democracy with human rights.

Serb in Croatia: The Croats can have their own state, but they have no right to take the Serbs in Croatia with them. We do not want to be ruled from Zagreb, which killed us during the war as an ally of Nazi Germany.

Bosniak: We are a nation with the same right as any other nation to have our own state through self-determination. We want to be governed neither from Istanbul, Vienna nor Belgrade, but from Sarajevo, and, in a broader European context, from Brussels. Our minorities can feel safe in a democracy with human rights.

Serb in Bosnia (BiH): The Bosniaks can have their own state, but they have no right to take the Serbs with them. We do not want to be governed from Sarajevo, which killed us during the war as an ally of Nazi Germany.

Croat in Bosnia (BiH): The Bosniaks can have their own state, but they cannot take the Croats in BiH with them. We are part of Croatia.

Serb in Serbia: Let the egoists go wherever they want to go. But no Serb will be governed from Zagreb, Sarajevo or Pristina, which killed us during the war as an ally of Nazi Germany and Fascist Italy.

Albanian in Kosova: We are a nation, with the same right as other nations to have our own state through self-determination. We want to be ruled neither from Istanbul nor Belgrade, but from Pristina and, in a broader European context, from Brussels. Our minorities can feel safe in a democracy with human rights.

Serb in Kosovo: The Albanians can have their own state, but they cannot take the Serbs with them. Independence or high-level autonomy.

Macedonian: We have the same right as all other nations to have our own state.

Albanian in Macedonia: The Macedonians can have their own state, but they cannot take the Albanians with them. Independence or high-level autonomy.

Montenegrin: We are a nation, with the same right as other nations to have our own state through self-determination. We want to be governed neither from Istanbul nor from Belgrade, but from Podgorica and, in a broader European context, from Brussels. Our minorities can feel safe in a democracy with human rights.

Albanian in Montenegro: Independence or high-level autonomy.

This summary, with 13 parties, is a simplification. But the Western simplification at the political level and in the media to 'the Serbs against the rest' was grotesque. The 1054 and 1095 fault lines between Catholics, Orthodox and Muslims (Slavic or Albanian) are historical realities. Most of it is unprocessed. Cynical leaders exploited that. And cynical outside parties (the Vatican, Austria, Germany, EU, Russia, Turkey, Saudi Arabia) exploited the cynical leaders' cynical exploitation of a horrible history. On top of that came the USA, which wanted, and got, a military base and an oil pipeline.

Conflict Worker: There are as usual three phases in conflict work:

- Get an overview of the goals – for internal and external parties.
- Divide the goals into valid/legitimate and invalid/ illegitimate.
- Build a bridge, a transcendence, between legitimate goals.

We are dealing here with a basic need: identity. One aspect of the identity of a human being is identification with the rulers. In other words, it is a question of the right to be ruled by one's own kind, not by others, even if these others constitute a benevolent, democratic majority. Individual human rights are good, but insufficient. On top of that comes the history of the Balkans, between the Habsburg (Vienna) and the Ottoman (Istanbul) empires. Invaded, occupied, annexed, by both for 900 years, as Afghanistan has been for the last 140 years. All empires ultimately decline and fall. But they leave behind catastrophes, and the 'Balkans' are blamed; a good reason for avoiding that word, using Southeast Europe instead.

What happened in Yugoslavia from 1990 onwards was a new chapter in the long history of violent intervention from the outside. At this point there are many goals, like re-establishing the Catholic Church, revenge for defeat in the First World War, for defeat in the Second World War, efforts to rebuild spheres of influence after Yugoslavia achieved independence under Tito. And then there are the perennial US military base and oil interests, aiming at control of Eurasia (and the rest of the world). The key to transcendence consists in seeing all the efforts by outside parties to fish in troubled waters as illegitimate, and to concentrate on the 13 inner goals.

But are these 13 goals compatible? Yes, with a formula within the limit of four words: *equal right to self-determination* – for all 13. The result would be an independent Slovenia which is what we have; an independent Croatia without the Serbian territories, possibly as a federation; an independent Bosniak country with Sarajevo as its capital; a Republika Srpska which itself decides its relationship to Serbia; the Croatian part of BiH integrated into Croatia; Serbia continuing as an independent country; an independent Kosovo/a as a federation with two Serbian cantons; the independent Macedonia we already have, but possibly as a federation, and an independent Montenegro, eventually also as a federation.

'Equal right to self-determination' conceives of the country as a set of Chinese boxes. The country has a right to self-determination, but that also applies to the minorities inside the country. And here we run into massive interests among the outside powers. Take France as an example: the country would not give the right of self-determination to its six minorities, and a key 'expert' in the handling of the Yugoslavia conflict was French. *Uti possidetis* this is called in international law, 'the borders remain the same'. That means minimum changes, with catastrophic results, in Africa for instance. As well as in Yugoslavia.

The outcome of all of this would be an ex-Yugoslavia with Slovenia as it is today, Croatia including the Croatian part of BiH, Kosovo/a, Macedonia and Montenegro as federations, two new countries (Republika Srpska and Kosova), and BiH reduced to the Muslim part – a Bosniak city-state plus its hinterland. And on top of this one would have to experiment with a soft community of these nations of the southern Slavs, neither too close nor too distant, based on brotherhood (*bratstvo*) and sisterhood, but not on unity (*jedinstvo*).

Today, only one problem has been solved, Slovenia. All the rest is worse than before. There are new layers of violence, trauma and hatred sedimented on top of the old ones, and more direction by outside parties than under Vienna and Istanbul. Where nothing has been solved the violence will recur, after some time.

Conclusion: Bad conflict work.

In 1992 TRANSCEND put forward the following proposal which was published in a number of places, as an example of opportunities lost, but not forever:

(1) A Conference on Security and Cooperation in Southeast Europe (CSCSEE), sponsored by the UN and OSCE; UNSC being too

remote, EU too partial, in addition to the London/Geneva conference process. All concerned parties (including sub-state, super-state and non-state) should be invited, with all relevant themes on the agenda; possibly lasting three to five years. Outsiders to the region should be present as observers with the right to speak, there being no disinterested outside states. One possible long-term goal: a Southeast European Confederation.

(2)   CSCSEE Working Groups on top priority areas to consider:
- Bosnia-Herzegovina as a tripartite confederation.
- Kosovo/a as a republic with the same status as for the Serbs in Krajina (not Knin) and with respect for Serbian history.
- Macedonia: a Macedonian confederation should not be ruled out, but can only emerge within a broader setting ([1] above).
- Ex-Yugoslavia: as a long-term goal, a confederation this time.

(3)   Increase UNPROFOR by ten or more, with 50 per cent women, creating a dense blue carpet to supervise truces and stabilise the situation. The soldiers must be adequately briefed with police, non-violence and conflict facilitation training, working together with civilian peacekeeping components. Avoid big power participation and powers with a history in the region.

(4)   A dense network of municipal solidarity with all parts of ex-Yugoslavia, for refugees, relief work, reconstruction: *Gemeinde gemeinsam*, *Cause commune*, Council of Europe.

(5)   Let a thousand local peace conferences blossom, support local groups with communication hardware, and the Verona Forum for Peace and Reconciliation on the Territory of Former Yugoslavia.

(6)   International Peace Brigades as Hostages for Peace, unarmed foreigners, professionals like doctors (WHO/IPPNW/MSF), working in threatened areas, communicating, dampening violence.

(7)   Intensify ecumenical peace work, building on non-violence and peace traditions in Catholic and Orthodox Christianity and Islam. Challenge hard-line religious institutions in the region.

(8)   Permanent contact among persons, groups and states working for peace within the state (1–3), municipal (4) and civil society (5–7) systems; let ideas flow. Have a 'Peace Ladies Conference' parallel to the London/Geneva warlords conferences; in the Palais des Nations.

(9) Demand professionalism from the media, less violence, elitism and bias; more focus on common people and peace efforts.

(10) In the spirit of future reconciliation,

- lift the sanctions, they hit the innocent and harden the conflicts;
- drop the War Crimes Tribunal except as moral individual judgment, there is no road to the future through revenge and punishment, adding to all the traumas, creating new martyrs;
- have inside and outside specialists search for an understanding of what went wrong and for positive past and present experiences that can inspire a common, even if more separate, future;
- build on the longing of the Yugoslav peoples rapprochement, none the less, in *bratstvo* (brotherhood) even if it should be with less *jedinstvo* (unity).

ISRAEL/PALESTINE: A MIDDLE EAST COMMUNITY

Conflict Worker: What is it you really want? What are the goals?

Israeli: We are a nation, with the same right as other nations again to have our own state, Israel, in our historical land, with security for Jews. A state to which all Jews can return with a capital in Jerusalem. A democracy with human rights.

Palestinian: We are a nation, with the same right as other nations to have our own state, Palestine, in our historical land, with security for Palestinians. A state to which they can return with a capital in East Jerusalem. A democracy with human rights.

That this is a simplification, that infinitely much more has been said, and even more can be said, we know. But let us try to look also at this conflict from above, get a bird's eye view, to see the major lines.

'Two nations, one territory' has five well-known outcomes:

(1) Unilateral I: One state, only Israel, 'transfer' of Palestinians.
(2) Unilateral II: One state, only Palestine, Israelis out.
(3) Negative transcendence: A third party (Ottoman, UK, UN) dominates.
(4) Bilateral compromise: Two-state solution, Israel and Palestine.
(5) Positive transcendence: Two nations enter symmetrically in one state:
- as a federation (model: Switzerland);
- as a unitary state (model: ?).

We have been through this at earlier stages in this book. Both (1) and (2) are non-starters, hopeless. How about the peace diagonal, (3) + (4) + (5)?

A third party can play a peace-keeping role for a short period. But (3) is clearly a formula from the past and is also hopeless.

What remains are (4) and (5). But a possible date for (5) lies far in the future, for instance the day when Bosniaks, Serbs and Croats are flourishing in the same country, living among each other, which may be approximately the same day as the Irish, the Welsh, the Scots and the English feel at home in the same unitary state.

What remains is (4). This outcome was given a major boost on 15 November 1988 when the Palestine National Council voted in favour of a two-state solution as a possibility, based on the West Bank, Gaza and East Jerusalem. An almost unparalleled willingness to compromise. But Israel continued its project with a state for all Jews; and Palestine wanted some return within Israeli borders. Both of them had a certain legitimacy. But not all legitimacy carries peace in its wake.

Imagine now that the parties yielded a little on these points, and that the 'Oslo process' was about the two-state solution and not only about a cease-fire with Palestine as some kind of Bantustan. At that point another reason comes up why a two-state solution for Israel-Palestine probably will not function. This book is an introduction to conflict work. Let us have a look at a closely related theme, the theory of peace and peace work.

If a major key to conflict is creativity, what then is a major key to peace? Only one word, please, no talk! That word is *equality*. It says a lot: equality among other things for the law, as equal justice, as reciprocity, symmetry. This is what men and women give each other in a good marriage, parents and children in a good family. Built into the 'peace diagonal' is an equality that cannot be found in the other two outcomes, hence the name. But that does not imply that all outcomes along that diagonal necessarily lead to peace. There may be other factors at work.

The parties may simply be too unequal. Take an example from Western Europe after the Second World War. Nazi Germany had been beaten, the guns had fallen silent. Peace? Not yet. But rather than suppressing and humiliating Germany, the French statesmen Jean Monnet and Robert Schuman had the elementary idea of founding peace on equitable cooperation. But cooperation between Germany and Luxemburg, or with the former German principality of Liechtenstein, would not have created peace. Formal equality between 'sovereign states' is not good enough. Germany was the biggest country, the other two among the smallest in Europe. Peace is based on reciprocity, which in turn is based on equality, equal rights and equal dignity. In the long run size matters. One can use the term balance, even a balance of power. But we are then thinking of the power of decision, the power of influence, the power of being constructive, of political, cultural and economic power, not only of the destructive military power of 'realists'.

In order to counterbalance Germany they brought in Be-Ne-Lux, Italy and that solid bastion of arrogance, France, in some kind of confederation, from the entry into force of the Treaty of Rome on 1 January 1958. There have been problems, but it has worked. A gigantic piece of successful peace work.

Germany had tried a unilateral solution, a *Neuordnung*, with itself at the centre, of course as stillborn as the unilateral 'roadmap' efforts of Spring 2003 being tried from Israel and USA. There was an element of a bilateral axis, Germany–France, that ultimately became a linchpin in the European Community, EC, and in the EU. But the solution was multilateral, not bilateral.

Conflict Worker: Like Western Europe, like the Middle East? For one who has followed this conflict for almost 40 years, with dialogues in many places, no more proof is needed that unilateral and bilateral outcomes will not work. A *Middle East Community*, based on Syria–Lebanon–Palestine (Sy-Le-Pal), Israel, Jordan and that solid bastion of arrogance, Egypt, might work. The transcendence is from uni-1 and bi-2 to multi-6.

Let us bring in from elementary peace theory a more precise version of reciprocity: *whatever you want for yourself you should also be willing to give to the other party, if he wants it*. An Israeli state? Then also a Palestinian state. A capital in Jerusalem? Then also for Palestine, in the West for one, in the East for the other. The right of return for Jews? So also for Palestinians. Where, and how many, can be negotiated. The Oslo process recognised no such reciprocity. In other words, it was not a peace process, but at best a cease-fire process. And even then it was a failure.

Israeli: A worse comparison than with Nazi Germany can hardly be imagined! In addition to that, that country had been defeated militarily.

Conflict Worker: Fundamentalist, Zionist Israel is now moving in the same direction. Israel has not suffered a military defeat, but like Germany has been defeated morally, by exhausting its moral capital. Security cannot be based on expulsion and repression, only on cooperation guided by equality.

Palestinian: Is our independence to be watered down in some kind of community?

Conflict Worker: It could also be strengthened by building good roads, transportation, trade, free flow across the borders, resurrecting the cultural community that once existed in the Middle East.

For Israel and Palestine there is no security at the end of the present road of violence; only increased violence and insecurity. Israel is now in the most dangerous period of its history: increasingly militarist, fighting unwinnable wars, increasingly isolated and with more and more enemies, exposed to violence, non-violence, and boycott from within and without, with the USA sooner or later making its support conditional on Israeli concessions.

The basic change in South Africa, from inside and outside may serve as a model:

- Israel's moral capital is rapidly depreciating, is probably negative in most countries and slowly changing in the USA.
- Israel is suffering from a *de facto* military coup, offering the electorate a choice of generals with limited agendas.
- Israeli violence and intransigence mobilise resistance and struggle in the Arab and Muslims worlds, if not in the sense of inter-state warfare, then in the postmodern sense of terrorism against Israeli state terrorism. Highly motivated volunteers willing to enter this struggle are in unlimited supply.
- Sooner or later this will include the 18 per cent Israeli Arabs.
- Sooner or later this may lead to massive non-violent struggle, like 100,000 Arab women in black marching on Israel.
- An economic boycott of Israel may come, like the one imposed on South Africa by NGOs and followed by local authorities which, as in South Africa, will be more important morally than economically.
- Again as in South Africa, US policy may change: economically, because Israel is becoming a liability, causing trade/oil problems with Arab countries no longer willing to see the USA as a neutral third party; with imminent boycotts and pressure to

disinvest; militarily, because Israel may commit the USA to highly dubious wars, and military bases are available elsewhere (Turkey, Kosovo/a, Macedonia); and politically, because Israel is a liability in the UN; the EU, and NATO allies, may not legitimise violent intervention. The USA may prefer a reasonable agreement to supporting a loser as they once did in Iran with the Shah, and in the Philippines with Ferdinand Marcos.

Could the following peace package be more attractive to reasonable people, if the context changes in the way outlined above?

(1) Palestine is recognised as a state following UN Security Council Resolutions 242 and 338; with 4 June 1967 borders with minor land transfers.
(2) The capital of Palestine is in East Jerusalem.
(3) A Middle East Community with Israel, Palestine, Egypt, Jordan, Lebanon, Syria as full members, with water, arms, trade regimes based on multilateral consensus; and an Organisation for Security and Cooperation in the Middle East with a broader base.
(4) The Community is supported by the EU, the Nordic Council and ASEAN financially and for institution-building expertise.
(5) Egypt and Jordan lease additional land to Palestine.
(6) Israel and Palestine become federations with two Israeli cantons in Palestine and two Palestinian cantons in Israel.
(7) The two neighbouring capitals become a city confederation, and are host to major regional, UN and ecumenical institutions.
(8) The right of return to Israel is accepted in principle, the numbers to be negotiated within the canton formula.
(9) Israel and Palestine have joint and equitable economic ventures, joint peace education and joint border patrols.
(10) Massive stationing of UN monitoring forces.
(11) Sooner or later a Truth and Reconciliation process.

Mediating a peace package should not be a country or a group of countries, but a respected person or group of such persons, with the EU, the Nordic Council and ASEAN as models.

In conclusion, some words written in 1993 about the Oslo Accords in the light of conflict and peace theory:

THE OSLO ACCORDS:
FROM A FLAWED PROCESS TO A FLAWED OUTCOME

I. Process

[1]   Extremists, meaning Hamas and Likud/Orthodox, were excluded. The agreement was between PLO and Labour/Secular-Modern; probably related to the Norwegian social democrat idea that 'reason lies in the middle'. This works in moderate Norway, but not when more than 50 per cent feel excluded. They also have peace concepts. When excluded they will announce themselves (killing Rabin, suicide bombs).

[2]   Peace actors/movements on both sides were also excluded. Intifadah and Peace Now were not even acknowledged; yet their action had been indispensable.

[3]   The USA, a major actor on the Israeli side, is not a signatory posing as a 'third party'. Was Oslo acting for the USA?

[4]   A general underestimation of polarisation inside Palestine and Israel; overestimation of the extent to which the accords are binding.

[5]   An unnecessary amount of secrecy, no dialogue with the general public.

II. Outcome; Structure

[6]   Lack of symmetry: the agreement does not define two states, but a state and an 'autonomy', which in fact exists at a lower level than the Bantustans in apartheid South Africa.

[7]   Not relational: the relations between the two sides are not spelt out militarily, politically, economically or culturally.

[8]   The Palestinian state not defined: there are glimpses, but not how that state would relate to Israel, militarily, politically, economically, culturally, e.g. as confederation (with Jordan?).

[9]   Excessive governmentalism and excessive institutionalism, no effort to weave the two civil societies together.

III. Outcome; Culture

[10] An underestimation, probably related to Norwegian secularism, of the strength of religion as a code informing people's behaviour, like the killing of a prime minister and the Hebron massacre at Purim, and the fourth stage of jihad – the Holy War.

[11] An underestimation of the sacredness of many sites in the area for the Jews (V. Jabutinski), only political/economic focus.

[12] An underestimation of the possibility of ecumenical work, between Jews, Muslims and Christians, to emphasise the positive, gentle aspects of the faiths and turn against the hard aspects.

These flaws were evident in August/September 1993, and the repercussions after the White House meeting are easily traced. The counter-argument is that the alternative was no agreement. But is it obvious that a seriously flawed agreement is better?

Conclusion: Bad conflict work.

MANDELA/DE KLERK/TUTU: TRUTH–RECONCILIATION–PEACE

South Africa 1994, almost three and a half centuries after the fateful arrival of Christian fundamentalists/terrorists as we would call them today, from the Netherlands, in 1652. The black people had won. The white people had capitulated after a cruel and unequal war, with terrorism and state terrorism and torture, the latter two supported by powerful countries in the West. The violence of the black people had mostly been directed against infrastructure like power stations; the violence of the white people against other human beings. It was impossible to build a future without processing, cleaning up that cruel past. The incumbent president, Nelson Mandela, and the outgoing President, F.W. de Klerk, were both lawyers and agreed that any process would have to be colour-blind.

Let us try to reconstruct their positions (based on conversations):

Mandela: We are now building democracy and a rule of law in South Africa. Perpetrators of violence have to be arraigned in court and punished if found guilty.

de Klerk: If that happens and most of the accused are white, then we can say goodbye to our peace agreement. The white people will never accept it. A far better solution would be amnesty, for everybody.

Mandela: If that happens, then we can say goodbye to our peace agreement. The black people will never accept that. Too many horrible things have happened to wipe out the truth. The voices of the victims and the bereaved have to be heard.

de Klerk: White people also believe they were fighting for a cause. They also demand that their side of the issue can be voiced without fear of punishment.

What Mandela wanted was a 'hard peace' with due process of law and punishment for political crimes, and that would above all target white people. What de Klerk wanted was a 'soft peace' with an amnesty for all. Both saw their point of view as a condition for a solid, sustainable peace. Mandela felt that de Klerk's line was an impossible start for South Africa as a state of law and order and a democracy, and that the victims had the right to let their suffering be known and deposited in the collective memory of the society. De Klerk was of the opinion that Mandela's line would challenge white people beyond breaking point and make them unreliable partners in a new social contract.

Concessions, law and order on the one hand, and amnesty for all on the other, were impossible. Withdrawal without any process, neither hard nor soft peace, was also impossible. The future could not be built on a rotten, unprocessed past. If they had chosen the evident compromise, Mandela for the worst perpetrators and de Klerk for the rest, then the world would not have taken a step forward. Fortunately, they did not do that. Through dialogue they were able to find a positive transcendence which will make legal history: amnesty in return for complete, public truth, and efforts toward genuine reconciliation.

The Truth and Reconciliation Commission administered the processes, conducted by a third peace genius, Archbishop Desmond Tutu. He challenged the victims to forgive the perpetrators if they told the whole truth about their misdeeds, apologised and in addition offered some compensation. And the state renounced its right to punish, an 'amnesty' in other words, if the conditions were fulfilled. Confession and apology might sound like little in return for forgiveness and amnesty for what were sometimes grotesque crimes. But precisely because they got off the hook without imprisonment, other forms of punishment were more effective: inner personal guilt and outer social sense of shame.

By coupling truth to reconciliation they were hoping for *healing* of the wounds in the mind and the spirit, leaving the body to the physicians, and with the hope that this would lead to *closure* of the conflict, like a closed book that will be opened only if the crimes are repeated. If you confess, you will be forgiven, but what you did will not be forgotten. Give compensation and you will not be the victim of revenge. But watch what you do. And it looks as if little or no revenge after these bloody deeds has taken place; there has been no private settling of scores.

The victims are no longer the forgotten party in the relation between state and perpetrator, with the cold comfort that the perpetrator now is suffering. The spiral of violence is broken because the parties are handling the issue directly, in face-to-face encounters. There is no doubt that this transforms their relationship in a way an abstract relationship built around the prison walls of the state cannot. But is such a transformation sustainable?

And what happened to justice? Are criminals really allowed to get off the hook that easily? Has peace building been bought through reconciliation at the expense of justice through punishment? Has one been sacrificed for the other?

The conflict between hard and soft peace has been transcended. But could it be that in its place another conflict has emerged, between the future and the past, at the expense of the past? Let us accept for the sake of argument that punishment does not deter crime in general. But isn't something unreleased, something not accounted for when justice has not been done?

That the traditional legal machinery of justice, deeply rooted in our societies, will make use of such arguments when they feel threatened that their social task may be taken better care of by others is evident. But that argument also has deep cultural roots. A *quid pro quo*, tit-for-tat, expressions found in all languages. Underlining this is probably some need for balance. Just as want a balance of positive values when we are buying and selling, we also want a balance of negative values, between trauma and punishment. The problem with guilt and shame is that the perpetrator can harden himself against both, and if he is really clever, may even transform detention in prison from suffering to joy. The problem is also that shame and guilt cannot be measured like a term of imprisonment or a fine. How can we know that we are administering a *quid pro quo*, tit-for-tat? How can we know that the shame of the perpetrator really matches the suffering of the victim?

One possible transcendence of this conflict might be that the Commission or any tribunal court sentences some perpetrators to a term of imprisonment under the assumption that they spend the time in prison preparing apologies to the victims, thinking through their compensation.

In South Africa transcendence was used not only to solve a conflict between two major politicians, but to find a solution which could be peace productive far beyond Mandela/de Klerk, and even far beyond South Africa in 1994.

*   *   *

Take a look at the micro-, meso- and macro-conflicts we have discussed. We have been dealing implicitly with strong persons backed by gender, class and race, with strong actors from capital and state, and with states and nations strongly backed by regions and civilisations. Quite often the status quo has been challenged. History reports that challengers are often challenged further by the struggle, and ultimately win. When they become part of the status quo, however, they may lose, becoming the victims of their own victory and success.

The words 'win' and 'lose' are deeply rooted in our culture, in games, sport, markets, court cases, wars. In a US senator's waiting room I once saw his diploma as a lawyer, a photo of him in full gear as a member of a US football team, and then as a young soldier in the Second World War in more modest gear. His model of how conflicts should be handled was crystal-clear: keep fighting until you win. A somewhat primitive way of deciding in a conflict.

This way we also produce many losers. Personal goals are suppressed, people lose and some people lose so often and so much that they start perceiving themselves as permanent losers. Good ideas get lost because their carriers are losing the struggle. Genders, generations, races, classes, nations, states, regions and civilisations are permanently suppressed, and sometimes exterminated or torn to pieces.

Let us take one of these examples, states with war as a decision mechanism, and look at it in more detail, against the backdrop of the Nuremberg and Tokyo tribunals. Wars have had such goods as land and cattle, women and slaves, plunder, human beings to be sacrificed, to be eaten, to incapacitate. War as 'the continuation of politics by other means' made the victory more political. The winner became a judge (usually Anglo-American) who punished the loser and sentenced him to compensation regardless of the complexity of the causes of the war; all of this according to a treaty which, in addition, often was referred to as a 'peace treaty'. And topping all of that came the effort to convert the defeated party to the political creed and system of the winner. Victory was supposedly not only over body and property, but over mind and spirit.

Let us say that the goal of the victor was a *hard peace*, with punishment, compensation and conversion. Let us say he hoped to eternalise the victory by punishing the population through compensation, the leaders through punishment and the future through conversion. And that the goal of the loser was a *soft peace* – OK, we lost, that's that. But if the capitulation was unconditional, as the USA always demands, he can hardly hope for a soft peace whether or not he is contemplating revenge and revanche. Can this contradiction between hard and soft treaties, between hard and soft peace, be transcended?

The second Versailles treaty of 1919 returned Alsace to the winner, France, after it had been transferred to the winner, Germany, in the first Versailles treaty of 1871. Then Germany won in 1940 and Alsace became Elsass, only to become Alsace again in 1945 when France won. At present this is a French region within the European Union. Let us wait and see what will happen next, all prior arrangements having been 'for eternity'. Versailles II also put military constraints on Germany and high reparations, but no additional punishment for the leaders among the German losers. The German Emperor abdicated, but generally people were punished and the leaders were released.

We usually, and probably correctly, associate this hard Versailles peace with Hitler's electoral victory in 1933. To avoid a repetition, the strategy in 1945 became to punish the leaders as war criminals and criminals against humanity, but not to punish the people, who were regarded as the victims of the leaders unless they had personally committed crimes. 'Punish the leaders, absolve the people' became a compromise between the hard and the soft peace after a war.

From 'booty, plunder' via 'compensation and punishment' to 'punish the leaders for their evil' there was a long road to travel. Of course, the leaders of old all belonged to the same aristocracy, whereas the new leaders came from or represented the 'dangerous classes'. But *transcendence* of the hard/soft conflict had to wait for the Truth and Reconciliation Commission in South Africa, and so far has been tried only in one country. Others, in Latin America, tried truth without reconciliation and the result was not convincing. A gift to humanity from South Africa!

That brings us back to the basic idea of transcendence: a constructive future-oriented approach to conflict, not destructive past-oriented. Punishment is destructive, focused on the past, and hopes for a preventive, deterrent effect for the future; a hypothesis poorly confirmed in countries, and even weaker among countries. The yearning for revenge and revanche is not extinguished by a punishment that rubs a few more grains of salt in the open wounds of defeat. The time horizon for revenge can be long. Nations may shame even elephants where memory is concerned.

As the Danish peace researcher Jan Öberg says, reconciliation = *saying goodbye to revenge*, and is an important part of the general theory of peace.

To summarise:

Conflict studies enable us to meet or approach conflicts with empathy, non-violence and creativity.

Peace studies enable us to prevent violence through equality and equity.

Reconciliation studies enable us to prevent future violence through healing and closure after the violence of the past.

Healing and closure are to violence what transcendence and transformation are to conflict: the problems dissolve. And the less structural violence there is in a society – with suppression, exploitation, divide and rule, exclusion – the less there is of cultural violence – with efforts to legitimise structural and direct violence – the more peace. Peace is also prophylaxis. Peace enables us to face new conflicts peacefully. Peace makes people great because they are less victims of structural and cultural violence between genders, generations and races, between classes, states and nations, between regions and civilisations.

Thursday: Mega-Conflicts Among Regions and Civilisations

As usual, first some words about the meaning of 'mega-conflicts'.

We started with persons, in and by themselves a construction. They are often conceived of as members of groups, or as representatives of categories with a shared culture, by which we mean nations if, in addition, they have a shared territorial attachment. If we put together a suitable combination of groups and categories, we get a society. If that society has a piece of land, we refer to it as a state and it may become a member of the United Nations. Within a state there is usually one nation that dominates the others.

And then we have arrived at the mega-level, level 4: the relations among regions with states as members, and among civilisations with nations as members, and the relation between these two. Level 3 was the relations among states and nations, and the relation between the two. Level 2 was the relation within states, in other words, among categories and groups. And level 1 was the relation within categories and groups, consisting of persons with their inner life and relations to each other. Constructions all the way, but rather useful constructions.

Regions as a rule consist of countries contiguous in space: East–West, during Cold War I (1949–89) and again during Cold War II (USA/NATO/AMPO against Eurasia). Regions can also be defined in terms of class, in other words power, of states: North–South.

Civilisations as a rule comprise nations that are contiguous in content: the different Christianities; the different Islams. As we shall see, Christianity thought of itself as an alternative for the whole world, for the 'pagans', the 'heathens'. That's an old habit, like the Chinese having four types of barbarians, North, South, East and West.

Once again, we should warn that states and nations may, to a greater or lesser degree, be members of the regions and civilisations that today are building blocks in an ever more globalised world. The lines of division are not always clear.

For the ten mega-conflicts we are exploring we can say much the same as for the macro-conflicts. Unsolved conflicts work like a brake, not only on states and their relations, but on the whole world. Rather than a dynamic world where humans, regardless of gender, generation, race, class, nation, state, civilisation and region, work together to create a life with dignity for all, the world is grinding to a halt, like an overheated engine without oil, exploding rather than moving humanity forward. Transcending and transforming means oiling the world machinery, as with US/UK–Iraq before, during and after the war of Spring 2003 – another very badly handled conflict.

Take Cold War I as an example. This came to an end without a big bang, thanks above all to the joint activities of ordinary people in the dissident movements in the East and the peace movements in the West, when they finally came together. Life under the nuclear sword of Damocles was not normal. People living in fear of a future that may become a radioactive wasteland are not free. And think of the lost creativity. Soviet communism was good in that basic material needs were the bedrock on which society was built. Western capitalism is good in that the market draws on the creativity of all. The two could have come together in a higher synthesis. Instead, we got a wild, borderless market, and millions, billions of jobless, hopeless, futureless, people.

Take the possible Cold War II, with the big three, Russia, India and China, caught in a US pincer movement. Nothing good will come out of that, only another nuclear threat and the squandering of resources we need for better purposes. The same applies to the North–South conflict we are all familiar with, closely related to the problems of sustainable development and globalisation. Life in a market economy on less than a dollar a day is not a life lived in dignity. Change the pay, change the system, or change both.

Half a millennium ago (behind mega-conflicts we often find mega-time) a Spanish pope launched what later became known as colonialism and imperialism, which brought unspeakable suffering and genocide. We do not accept that any person should steal another's property, and have gradually come to accept that no person can steal another person and make her/him a slave. For a very long time, however, we accepted that one country could steal another country, along with everything in it: humans as well as things. Even Norway, with no colonies, made good money by becoming the transport agent in the system. This is important because there will always be somebody profiting from conflict, even from violence, and for that reason standing in the way of transcendence and transformation.

Behind these international class conflicts another civilisation conflict, between Christianity and Islam, is lurking. Islam once attacked and occupied Christian Spain. The Christians went one step further and declared a brutal war against Islam, the Crusades, which lasted two centuries. There is no peace treaty, 'only' millions of people waiting – some perhaps hoping – for something to happen, the Big Holy War, or the Big Holy Peace. And then Something Big did happen, 11 September 2001 – big because it happened in the big USA, in Washington and New York. At least half of humanity has been touched by this as we wait for further acts of terrorism and state terrorism in this combination of class and civilisation conflict, fuelled by a vicious cycle of violent retaliation, and then more retaliation.

But then there are the high points – Mandela/de Klerk and Gandhi. For them unsolved conflict and violence waste human resources. They wanted to bring regions, races, countries out of the backwaters and into the flow of history. For good and for bad. In the future many new conflicts are waiting for us. Better be well prepared.

COLD WAR I: POLARISED DIALOGUE ABOUT DEPOLARISATION

We are back to the Cold War with its enormous problems and contradictions. The parties were given stupid ornithological names – hawks, owls and doves, aggressive birds known for their pecking order. Our concern here is polarisation/depolarisation, with clear positions.

Polarisation: In the struggle of 'democracy against dictatorship', and 'anti-fascism against imperialism', there can be no compromise. We have to play hard ball and arm ourselves until the other party gives in or loses the war.
Depolarisation: Cold war = polarisation + the arms race, and that can lead to a war which could bring an end to humanity, 'Arms race or Human race'. We have to depolarise and disarm.

These diametrically opposed positions were found not only within each bloc and each country, in the Eastern bloc, but more privately, in churches, universities, etc. Polarisation was also found within single individuals, at the top; in the USA even if the USA talked more about war and polarisation and the Soviet Union more and more about peace and depolarisation.

One compromise quite often resorted to was the summit meeting. Dramatic, because the logic of polarisation was totally opposed to any such meeting. The enemy has only one idea in mind, defeat us! For that reason we have to prevent him from exercising any influence on us at all (polarisation) and be strong enough to deter him and win any war should it come (armament, modernisation). We can trust only our own leaders. Hence summit meetings.

Expectations of what these meetings could produce far exceeded the outcomes. In a research project for the Council of Europe in 1967 in 19 foreign offices from Washington to Moscow, and from Oslo to Athens, the present author proceeded somewhat differently. Dialogues were organised with only one party at a time, and the theme was how Europe could be better organised for cooperation. A number of cooperation topics and organisation models were discussed, and the dialogues proceeded over that entire field, but with only one person, as a rule the head of the political section of the foreign ministries.

A model of cooperation that enjoyed a very high level of consensus was the United Nations Economic Commission for Europe. The problem, however, was that these high officials were more concerned with security. Some proposed pure polarisation until the other side gave up. Others were in favour of polarisation combined with mutual and balanced disarmament. Still others were in favour of unilateral disarmament. Very few, almost nobody, showed any interest in solving the conflict between capitalism and socialism. At best they were hoping for convergence towards a point in the middle, as a compromise process.

Not much was needed to combine these two in a concrete proposal in 1967: a permanent United Nations Security Commission for Europe, before the Helsinki conference moved exactly in that direction (without the United Nations, however); open to all security problems, and for all countries in the system. But within the framework of polarisation, with the Cold War conflict sedimented in the construction and the agenda of the Commission.

The Council of Europe was hostile even to this modest idea:

'A Monsieur Galtung has proposed that we shall sit down and discuss the problems of Europe with communists! I would like to say one thing: anybody who says anything like that is himself a communist!!'

so said the French committee chairman. The history of how this idea played a certain role at the end of the Cold War has been told elsewhere, in *Searching for Peace*.

The transcendence consisted in using a polarised dialogue to promote depolarisation, by finding something in the interest of both sides. The Commission would differ from a summit meeting because all countries would participate and at a lower level. And it would differ from disarmament conferences by being more conflict- and less arms-oriented.

As in the Ecuador/Peru conflict the transcendence was easily understood. Again there was a certain fatigue and a certain sense of shame. The basis for the proposal was a broad series of dialogues, involving all parties. This was the project where the TRANSCEND method was born. And the seed sown bore fruit two decades later.

COLD WAR II: A DEMOCRATIC UN AS TRANSCENDENCE

'The real task for the US army is to make the world safe for our economic and cultural assault. Towards these goals there will be a fair amount of killing', writes a head of planning in the Pentagon.
(Susan George, 'The Corporate Utopian Dream',
The WTO and the Global War System, Seattle, November 1999)

Author: World hegemony + state violence = geo-fascism.

The USA has a geopolitical agenda with its roots in the nineteenth century, now being transported into the twenty-first century through the global expansion of NATO eastward (so far with Polish, Czech and Hungarian membership) and AMPO, the USA–Japan Security Treaty, westward. As seen from the north-western corner of the world power centre, the USA, the Eurasian continent is indeed the very source of geopolitical evils. Latin America is a backyard and is easily controlled. Africa is insignificant. But for the USA, Eurasia is the cauldron out of which come populism, war and terrorism, billions of coloured people with a different outlook on life, and fundamentalism. In addition, South Asia has two new nuclear powers, India and Pakistan. Central Asia has oil and bridgeheads for the USA. And then there is Southeast Asia which, until recently, enjoyed very strong economic growth. All of them in Eurasia.

The same certainly holds for Russia with White Russia and Ukraine, and for China, not to mention the problematic Eurasian peripheries, the Korean Peninsula and Southeast Europe. 'A global nation with global interests' (USA) has its reasons for bringing the alliances up to fundamental, explosive fault lines: between the Catholic–Protestant and the Slavic–Orthodox in Europe, and between Shinto Japan and the rest of Asia. A totally defensive Japan is a threat to no one. But deep cooperation with the most mobile military power in the world sends a different signal to its neighbours. The double expansion, with 'anchors' on both sides of Eurasia (the USA–Turkey–Israel alliance and the USA–Japan–South Korea alliance), follow logically from Roosevelt's directive JCS570/2, the 'Base Bible'. A look at the map shows us how the double expansion can be perceived as a pincer movement against the big three, Russia, India and China, with 40 per cent of the world's population.

Cold War I was between the USA/NATO/AMPO and the Soviet Union/WTO (the Warsaw Pact). The Soviet Union and WTO were dissolved; the USA, NATO and AMPO were reinforced. This could have been the introduction to a negative transcendence, neither WTO, nor NATO/AMPO and general disarmament. But the interpretation held by the USA was victory, and it was going to reap the fruits.

Cold War II is between USA/NATO/AMPO and Russia/India/China. At the time of writing (2003) the USA has cleverly manoeuvred the other three to give priority to the struggle against Muslim autonomy (Chechnya, Kashmir, Xinjiang).

This won't last long. Cold War II is a strong conflict formation.

If Russia and China resolve their conflicts, if Russia reaches new agreements with India, China with Pakistan, and lines up with what the USA calls rogue states (Serbia, Libya, Iraq, Iran, North Korea), then the continent will be unified against the USA/NATO/AMPO. A minor incident along the problematic border between Poland and Ukraine, or in the Korean peninsula in the North Korea/South Korea/Japan triangle, and these fault lines will erupt like volcanoes, with nuclear powers on all sides and, practically speaking, no neutral countries in between to serve as buffers as Finland–Sweden–Austria–Yugoslavia did for Cold War I.

Eurasia under the USA, Brzezinski's 'grand chess game', is as insane as the USA dominated by Eurasia. The old compromise, 'spheres of interest', is better, under the assumption that the USA is withdrawing from what they have meticulously built in Eastern Europe, the Middle East and East Asia. The whole world as a sphere of interest is also known as megalomania. A positive transcendence in the sense of a world dictatorship under the five great powers, the USA–EU–Russia–

India–China is too reminiscent of the Security Council, with four Christian and one Confucian country, and the 56 Muslim countries members of the UN unrepresented. A much better transformation would be through negative transcendence with no big powers:

(1) Abolish the veto power, expand the Security Council into something representative, with the European Union and the Organisation of the Islamic Conference (OIC) as members.
(2) A United Nations People's Assembly (UNPA) with one representative per million inhabitants in the member countries, directly elected through a free and secret ballot. As in East Greenland, a 'negative transcendence' may often work positively, and a 'positive transcendence' may work negatively – from some value point of view.
(3) And then as a possible first step: United Nations out of the USA and USA out of the United Nations if they cannot accept world democracy at the state and people levels.

NORTH–SOUTH:
BASIC NEEDS AS GOALS, STATE–CAPITAL AS THE MEANS

Conflict Worker: A modern society rests on three pillars: State, Capital and the Civil Society (local authorities and non-governmental organisations). All of them want 'development'. What does that goal mean for each of you?

State: Power-political, economic, military and cultural growth.

Capital: Wealth, turnover and growth.

Civil Society: Basic needs for all, dignity and growth.

Conflict Worker: Whatever it means, you all seem to want more growth. But if we get ever more State, Capital and human beings in this materially finite world, then sooner or later we will bang our heads against an outer limit. Is there also an inner limit, a minimum, a floor?

State/Capital: No, we want more!!

Civil Society: Yes, there is: basic needs.

Conflict Worker: In other words survival, with well-being, freedom and identity. We humans managed for quite a long time without State and Capital, but never without Nature. Nature managed quite well without all three. In other words, first come the needs of Nature, then of human beings, and finally of State and Capital. We can hitch the concept of development to Nature and human beings so that both can unfold, like flowers. Human beings need food, water, air, clothes, housing, sleep, health, sex, children and education. Freedom and identity are built into structure and culture and do not cost a lot. The key to survival is found in conflict transformation, so that conflicts do not lead to lethal violence. That's not very expensive either.

But State has a tendency to see power in expensive palaces, monuments, armies. And Capital has to sell and buy things, achieve turnover, in order to become rich. They are both strong, and they can take what they need from Nature and human beings. The result, however, is misery and death.

The problem is not the relation between North and South, but the relation between State–Capital and Nature–human beings. State–Capital is so strong in the North that they can even take resources from Nature–human beings in the South. But that is politics and power, not geography. In addition, State and Capital are better at living in symbiosis, with Capital paying taxes to State in return for protection by the military and police. Humans and Nature are not that good at symbiosis in today's society.

We have a society where State–Capital dominate at the same time as Nature is depleted and polluted and human beings are suffering. We have to go back to the period before the early beginnings of State and Capital to find the opposite trend. On the other hand, nobody will deny that State and Capital have been very helpful in promoting general growth. The concept of development cherished by economists, gross national product per capita, is a bookkeeping concept adopted from business. And basic needs were brought into the picture only a decade ago through the United Nations' Index for Human Development and its *Human Development Report*.

Positive transcendence would be a social contract with State and Capital that places the satisfaction of citizens' and customers' basic needs at the centre. Human beings and their needs would be the measure of all things, not abstractions like the power of the State and the wealth of Capital. But for this to happen human beings have to control State and Capital. A compromise would, as a minimum, be a reasonable relation between the salaries of State ministers and Capital directors on the one hand, and workers on the other. But negative transcendence, neither State–Capital nor Nature–human beings, would be the end of history.

What happened to 'North–South'? A geographical orientation has made us believe that the gap between poor and rich can be reduced if State–Capital in the North cooperates with State–Capital in the South in a 'war against poverty'. But that 'war' usually leads to the rich in State and Capital becoming even richer. In reality it becomes a war against the poor and against Nature.

Positive transcendence between State–Capital in the North and State–Capital in the South by creating still more multilateral organisations is not the solution either. Nor does it help if one dominates the other. Compromise in the form of massive transfers from State in the North to State in the South (development assistance) will enrich the State in the South, and sometimes help human beings–Nature. But the transfers from Capital in the South to Capital in the North are much more massive.

A solution to this conflict is the negative transcendence through direct cooperation between Civil Society in the North, and Civil Society in the South. Local communities and their production for the basic needs of human beings will have to be strengthened, and this can best be done through cooperation between non-governmental organisations, supported, but not co-opted, by State–Capital. The Porto Alegre process points in that direction.

GLOBALISATION: YES, FROM BELOW, DEMOCRATICALLY

In the process of globalisation we see clearly what happens when Capital controls the State, and the two together control human beings in meetings behind closed doors. Capital gets the world as its *borderless market* and eradicates local markets; Capital takes over the economic activity of the State through *privatisation*; misery increases because human beings can no longer get what they need for their basic needs such as food through work, but have to get it via money, *monetisation*; and can get money only through jobs that are non-existent because of *high labour productivity*. Competition between Capital and Capital gives lower prices, but also higher unemployment by reducing labour costs. Together these four factors lead to less purchasing power among people, bankruptcies in Capital and deflation. This holds for both North and South, but the South is more vulnerable. So we get enormous protests against elite meetings held behind closed doors, and the World Social Forum in Porto Alegre, in January 2003 with 100,000 participants and 1,700 seminars.

The gap between poor and rich is widening. The number of ecological, economic, political, military and cultural refugees is also increasing, possibly with one billion human beings on the road by the year 2030, and steadily growing 'security' walls around and within rich countries. Low or negative taxes, 'incentives', reduce the income of states and local communities at the same time that some people in Capital are becoming enormously wealthy.

An ever-growing gap in buying power will lead to speculation, which in turn will lead to crashes on the stock exchanges when stock prices are out of touch with reality. The International Monetary Fund is like a physician with only one cure: independence of the companies of the State (privatisation, lower taxes, devaluation), from the workers (flexibility, contract work) from the country (repatriation of profit), from human beings (no subsidies for basic needs, no taxation on luxury products). A totally illegitimate system pitted against the total legitimacy of the basic needs of human beings.

A legitimate globalisation would mobilise both genders, all generations, all races, all classes, all nations and all states in an effort to work jointly for a life lived in dignity for all. Only an improved United Nations can do anything like that and has already done a lot. Instead, we have a caricature, driven by mainly middle-aged males, by and for white people, by and for the economic upper class, Anglo-Saxon with a couple of other nations participating, and the USA dominant, through the World Bank, the International Monetary Fund and the World Trade Organisation.

In a conflict like that, between legitimate and illegitimate, alternatives are needed, not transcendence:

- *Reinventing the local community*: production for basic needs locally, or in a confederation of local communities, to guarantee that they are met, and in order to get such positive side effects as local creativity, local networks and less pollution because of shorter transportation distances.
- *Reinventing the state*: production of standard goods within the state, or a confederation of states, in order to get the positive side effects, reduce pollution and ensure better distribution,

and in addition to make public space safe, accessible to all, aesthetic and shared.

- *Reinventing the company*: companies have to give priority to production for basic needs at accessible prices, assume more social responsibility and then be rewarded ('girlcott') or punished (boycott) accordingly by the customers.
- *Reinventing economic theory*: by basing it on basic needs, satisfaction, not on demand and profit.
- *Reinventing civil society*: a major task will be dialogue with local authorities, the state and companies so that reward and boycott of companies can be organised through increased consumer consciousness, in a free market.
- *Reinventing the media*: by liberating them from all types of censorship promoted by Capital and State interests, and by directing reporting on economic affairs towards basic needs and distribution more than toward stock exchanges, profit and growth.
- *Reinventing global governance*: through massive taxation of speculation, and by having satisfaction of basic needs as a basic human right. And by having a United Nations People's Assembly, directly elected as a democratic world parliament.

SUSTAINABLE DEVELOPMENT: HUMANITY AS TRANSCENDENCE

A flower develops by unfolding its potential, not by growing to become the biggest flower. A human being does the same, not by putting on ever more weight to become the heaviest human being. Neither the flower nor the human being will grow forever. Development has its limits.

What about humanity? Humanity is also developing, unfolding its potential for good and for ill. We do not know where this is going to lead us. But don't we have a duty to let that process continue? If not necessarily with eternal life for humanity on this earth as a goal, but at least for a while? In other words, sustainable development to secure the possibility of life on earth for future generations, and the possibility for humanity of reaching even further goals. We are of the opinion that we humans have the capability of reprogramming ourselves for the better, and for that reason also a duty of self-preservation. If we were of the opinion that we were heading irreversibly downhill, that Good had been killed by Evil (as Baldur was by Loki in Nordic mythology), then euthanasia would be a better solution than sustainability.

A voice from the present: But the future never did anything for me!
A voice from the past: If we had all been thinking like you, then not even you would have existed!
A voice from the future: We are the road you have to travel for further development!

Conflicts among generations are acted out through time, diachronically. Conflict theory and practice are mostly about conflicts between parties coexisting in time, synchronically. Each generation has its own well-being as its basic goal. Each generation tries to meet its own basic needs; that's already in the world. We suffer from presentism.

The conflict arises when a generation stands in the way of future generations through inconsideration:

- *Economically,* by polluting and depleting the environment.
- *Militarily,* by stimulating chains of violence in the search for revenge and glory.
- *Politically*, through untransformed conflicts and irreversible action.
- *Culturally*, by accepting cultures with such consequences.

The concept of sustainability transcends economics and ecology and points to something beyond. We are talking about handing over to future generations a world in good order, with an environment with diversity and symbiosis, with human beings less deeply wounded by violence and less distorted by the desire to rule through violence, with conflicts transformed so that they can be handled non-violently and creatively, and world cultures that privilege such messages. Efforts at reconciliation will also be very important in this connection.

But what happens in fact is pollution and the depletion of resources, increasing violence, so that the wisdom with which conflicts are handled seems to decrease, and the cultures that counteract all of this are sidelined. The burden of unsolved problems imposed on future generations will increase, with the exception that there is a better material standard of living for the upper classes of the world. The prognosis is increased violence, massive immigration into sparsely settled areas and the four evils from Revelation 6:1–7: conquest, war, famine, pestilence. What can we set up against this egotism and lack of solidarity with future generations, and against short-term perspectives blocking the welfare of future generations?

The advice from American Indians, 'think through the consequences of your action for the next seven generations', is excellent, and points to what today is referred to as future studies. But we are talking about perspectives far beyond the narrow time horizon for the majority of such studies. And such studies can also be the pretext for a lack of consideration by identifying some carrying capacities strong enough to instil faith in the ability of the world to carry more pressure. To be on the safe side insight into tomorrow should be related to solidarity over time, in addition to solidarity in space, with the here and now.

One way of training would be in a household (*oikos*) where three or four generations live closely together, so closely that solidarity becomes an everyday necessity. Solidarity also applies retrospectively, to parents and grandparents, something that's easily forgotten when the emphasis is so single-mindedly on future-directed solidarity so that old people are dumped in old people's homes, even against their will.

Another approach would be a change to the balance of power in society, and in world society, in the direction of groups better known for their wisdom in the sense of having a more holistic perspective, a more global orientation and more respect for basic human needs – above all, with a longer time perspective. This should point towards older people and towards women. Women today are heading into positions of power and the older generation is heading in the other direction. The first trend should be encouraged and the second reversed.

Massive education and mobilisation of religious, eternity-oriented organisations as carriers of solidarity across generational gaps would also enter the picture. Sustainability needs metaphysical legitimation. Short-term, egoistic cost-benefit analysis leads to inconsideration because the terms of trade between generations are so asymmetrical. Future generations cannot do anything for us, whereas we can decide their being, non-being or well-being.

Or so we think. But we have already indicated the need for metaphysics. The positive transcendence between our generation and future generations is located in a transcending notion, *humanity*. It is not true that the future generation has done nothing for us. We give them our experience. By receiving that gift they accept us, and the more they do so the more we have to offer. Try to give Christmas gifts without anybody receiving them and you will see better how humanity is an organism of reciprocity stretched out through time. We need each other, past–present–future. We need faith in humanity.

CHRISTIANITY AND THE HEATHENS: THE TRUTH THAT WAS FALSE

I quote from one of Western civilisation's most important and for that reason least known documents, the papal bull *Inter Caetera* of 4 May 1493. The Pope, Alexander VI, was Spanish, and he was praising our 'very dear son/daughter in Christ', *los reyes catolicos*, Ferdinand and Isabella, for spreading:

- Christianity, so 'that barbarous nations be overthrown and brought to the faith':
- as witnessed with so much glory to the Divine Name in your recovery of the kingdom of Granada from the yoke of the Saracens;
- you chose our beloved son, Christopher Columbus, to make diligent quest for these remote and unknown mainlands and islands through the sea, where hitherto no-one had sailed; and
- discovered certain very remote islands and even mainlands that hitherto had not been discovered wherein dwell very many peoples living in peace going unclothed and not eating flesh disposed to embrace the Catholic faith and be trained in good morals
- built a fortress fairly equipped, wherein he has stationed in garrison certain Christians, companions of his, who are to make search for other remote and unknown islands and mainlands. In the islands and countries already discovered are found gold, spices, and very many other precious things
- bring under your sway the said mainlands and islands with their residents and inhabitants and bring them to the Catholic faith.

Whereupon He, Alexander VI, assigns to *los reyes catolicos*

- and your heirs and successors, kings of Castile and Leon, forever

- all rights, jurisdictions, and appurtenances, all islands and mainlands, found and to be found, discovered and to be discovered;
- we appoint you lords of them with full and free power and *jurisdiction of every kind* (italics ours).
- Let no one, therefore, infringe, or with rash boldness contravene, this our recommendation, exhortation, requisition, gift. grant, assignment, constitution, deputation, decree, mandate, prohibition and will. Should anyone presume to attempt this, be it known to him that he will incur the wrath of Almighty God and of the blessed apostles Peter and Paul.

In short: the Earth belongs to God, the Pope is the administrator of God's will, and he has the mandate to delegate all jurisdiction to the kings of Spain. In doing so, Alexander VI legitimised for a long-lasting posterity the enormity of colonialism and imperialism, and created a protracted conflict between those who suffer under this illegitimate papal bull, and those who do not revoke the bull.

Author: This does not call for transcendence, but for an alternative, a soft Christian papal bull, for instance:

We, Alexander VI, servant of the servants of the Christian God, to the Catholic Kings of Castile, Leon, Aragon and Granada:

To us has been given a remarkable gift: to travel by ship, guided by the Almighty's stars, across vast oceans, to distant islands and mainlands different from ours in Europe, and above all inhabited by people and peoples different from us in Europe.

We thank you, our Mother and Father God, the Son, the Holy Spirit, for this wonderful opportunity given us to be enriched by encountering Others, engaging them, celebrating the diversity of us humans, of our beloved animals and plants, of the seas and coasts and mountains under the magnificent sky, illuminated by the God Sun.

We shall learn from their Truths, from how they see the world and all the miracles dwelling therein. We shall offer them our Truths for them to taste and judge by their fruits. And together we shall all move forward, spiritually, materially, learning from each other through the word, *dia logos*, through exchange of our products. What a wonderful, challenging opportunity for us all to explore deeper truths than any single segment of humanity can ever develop alone.

We, Alexander VI, servant of the servants of the Christian God, direct you, Kings of Castile, Leon, Aragon and Granada, to

- approach these peoples, discovered by us and to be discovered by us, in deep humility and respect never imposing upon them, by any kind of power, by force or threat of force, by gifts or promise of gifts but engage in friendly exchanges guided by reciprocity if they so want. If they do not want, leave them in peace, tell them where you can be found should they become of an other mind. And you may ask them what could change their mind, to understand their reasons not to take us on as we want to take them on;
- learn from these peoples. To us has been given the understanding that they live in peace, walk naked and do not eat meat. Try to learn from them the knowledge and wisdom that has guided them toward a life in peace, so sorely missing in our part of the world. Is it in any way related to the other two points? Ask them humbly to be your teachers in the difficult art of harmony;
- never build any fortified tower or garrison, but ask them for the permission to dwell among them, at your risk, not theirs.

You expelled the Muslim Saracens, because they had unlawfully occupied your land, and the Jewish Moriscos. I direct you to invite back as many Muslims and Jews as want to return, to settle in your lands, to enrich you by having different ideas of the message in the Holy Book, and to continue the wonderful dialogues among the Abrahamitic religions in Alhambra, in Granada, with the hope of reaching ever higher, and ever deeper in the understanding of the Creation that unites us all.

Problem: The papal Christianity of 1493 could not have produced anything like this. But Pope John Paul II, after the attempt on his life gave him a new spirituality, could perhaps have done so. And how about the next pope? And the one after that?

CHRISTIANITY AND ISLAM: THE TRUTHS DO NOT EXCLUDE EACH OTHER

Conflict Worker: How is it that you both think that you possess the only true teaching?

The Hard Christian:	Because God the Father revealed himself to Moses and gave him the Laws, The Ten Commandments and sent His Son to the earth so that we could attain eternal life through the faith in Him. Islam rejects the Christ.
The Hard Muslim:	Because Allah revealed himself to Mohammed, the Prophet and gave him the Qur'an. *Musa* (Moses) and *Isa* (Jesus) are Messengers, *Nabi*, but not the One True Prophet, *Rasul*. The only true God is Allah, and Mohammed is His Prophet.
Conflict Worker:	Yours are revelation religions. Judaism was the basis for Christianity, and both were incorporated into Islam?
Unison:	NO! Our revelation is the only true one!
Conflict Worker:	Could I have some softer voices, please?
The Soft Christian:	Apart from the teachings about Christ we are rather similar.
The Soft Muslim:	Apart from the teachings about Christ we are rather similar.

On 27 November 1095, in the French city of Clermont, Pope Urban II called for Christianity to launch a crusade to 'liberate' the Holy Land. In 1291 the Crusades came to an end and the Christians withdrew. But there was never any real peace treaty. The Crusades became an example of the use of religion to justify a war that also had political and economic aspects. This became sedimented in the collective memory of the Christian Crusades and as a 'Gulf syndrome' in Iraq, which had the most cruel experience of the Crusades, the Baghdad massacre of the Muslims in 1258 by Hulaku, the grandson of Genghis Khan, with the blessing of the pope; which was repeated in 1991 and again in 2003 (but this time without the blessing of the pope).

Conflict Worker: We are dealing with two rather similar religions. The hard, the extremists, both want to dominate alone. The soft indicate that they can tolerate the other's teaching, side by side, with a church here and a mosque there, perhaps also with a dialogue. Then there is a very clear negative transcendence, a neither/nor, well known as secularism or conversion to other religions, which is beyond doubt also inspired by the cruelty of religious wars, like the atrocities of the Thirty Years War, 1618–48. But where is the positive transcendence?

Nine centuries later, on 26–27 November 1995, a dialogue was convened at the Swiss Institute for Development in Biel/Bienne, bringing together leading representatives of the Christian and Islamic faiths: Ayatollah, Professor Mohammad Taghi Jafari, Tehran; Sheikh Ahmad Kuftarou, Grand Mufti of Syria, Damascus; Nuncio, Archbishop K.J. Rauber, Bern; Metropolitan Damaskinos, Bishop of the Orthodox Church, Geneva; and scholars and clerics. The author, peace researcher, and director of TRANSCEND, was convenor.

Pope John Paul II sent his blessings and a message to the symposium through Cardinal Angelo Sodano, Secretary of State of the Holy See: 'It is opportune to reflect on these events, in order to draw vital lessons for today. His Holiness renews the call of the Second Vatican Council which urged that a sincere effort be made to achieve mutual understanding, so that Christians and Muslims would together preserve and promote peace, liberty, social justice and moral values to the benefit of all.'

Communiqué:
'The adherents of Islam and Christianity propose the following to members of their respective faiths and all others:
  - to try to understand other religions in the way their followers understand themselves, as a condition for true dialogues;
  - to develop school material in history, civic education and religious education, particularly material about the two religions, acceptable to all parties;
  - not to abuse the freedom of speech when speaking and writing about other religions;
  - to work together to identify, develop further and put into practice an inspiring ethic of peace, liberty, social justice, family values, human rights and dignity, and nonviolent forms of conflict resolution;
  - to establish permanent inter-religious councils to further mutual respect and understanding;
  - to cooperate across religious borders in Bosnia to reconstruct the country;
  - to discuss with people in the media more responsible, peace-promoting forms of journalism.

On this day of the ninth centenary of the call for the Crusades, we call upon Christians, Muslims and all others, to go beyond mere tolerance. We must open our hearts and minds to each other. Instead of sensing danger when somebody is different let

us be filled with joy at the opportunity to learn, to enrich and be
enriched, to live in peace and create peace. Like everything else the
two largest religions in the world are also subject to development.
While keeping the basic message of devotion let us find new ways,
acts and words. It is in the spirit of freedom of interpretation of
one's own religion that genuine respect for other religions can
evolve. Let the next 900 years and beyond be an era of active peace
built in our hearts and our minds, and enacted in our deeds.'

It fits the picture that apart from a meeting of historians in
Clermont, the dialogue in Biel was the only conference on this theme
in Europe, as opposed to several in Muslim countries. It also fits that
the media were totally indifferent to it. With the seven concrete
points above, particularly numbers 5 and 11, September 2001 might
perhaps have been avoided.

Conflict Worker: From the point of view of conflict theory this is only
a compromise, tolerance, side by side; a meeting between the soft and
the not-so-hard. The formulations point in the direction of positive
transcendence ('We have to open our hearts and our souls'; 'Let us
be filled with the joy at having a chance to learn, to enrich and be
enriched'), but there is no clear, sustainable both/and unless I say,
as the French say, '*Je prends mon bien où je le trouve*' – 'I take what I
need where I find it.' For instance, I could take three excellent ideas
from Christianity:

- the distinction between *peccato* and *peccatore*, between sin and
  sinner;
- forgiveness and love rather than rejection and hatred;
- each individual's personal responsibility, not cowering behind
  others.

And I could take three excellent ideas from Islam:

- zakat, give directly to those in misery;
- Qur'an 8:61: if the other side is leaning towards peace, do you
  likewise;
- Sala'am–Islam–Muslim: submit yourself to the message of
  peace.

In doing so I have indicated six guidelines for my own life. Others would make different choices and draw on other sources of wisdom to get a more solid foundation on which to stand. What matters here is rejecting the idea that mixing, eclecticism, amalgams are a sin and rejecting the fundamentalist way of looking at the two teachings, seeing them as each other's contradiction, so that learning from both is a symptom of mental disorder. Nonsense. It is exactly in combining, in the capacity to draw on the wisdom of the whole world, that true transcendence is located.

THE USA, THE WEST AND THE REST:
BASIC NEEDS, THEN TRADE, RELIGION

To the USA and the West '11 September 2001' was an *event* that heralded a new era. Like the 'shot in Sarajevo' of 28 June 1914, 9/11 served to release a massive 'war against terrorism'. 28 June 1914 did the same for the First World War, as if these were the only reasons. Behind these events the West saw Evil, Osama bin Laden and Gavrilo Princip. Evil is seen as its own explanation, cause and effect coalesce by evil realising itself. There is no need for any further explanation. The therapy is obvious: identify, locate and crush evil through American anti-terrorism and Austrian anti-Serbianism. The West has nothing to do with this; only the Other, the Evil. The West is innocent.

A little child, quoted on US television immediately after 9/11, said what needed to be said about such nonsense: 'What have we done since they hate us so much that they do something like that?' Reality is better understood as a part of a causal chain; long chains, many of them, criss-crossing, biting their own tails. But chains, where all causes have causes, and all effects have effects. One example would be the chain of retaliation according to the principle that violence breeds violence. Nothing is its own cause.

But this is too general. The perpetrators were Arabs, most of them from Saudi Arabia, and the targets were specific buildings:

Saudi Arabian, Wahhabite: They offended our holy land economically and militarily, introducing other religions, over-consumption and a corrupt royal family!

American: The agreement between Roosevelt and Ibn Saud in 1945 gave us access to oil in return for protecting the royal family. And as for

	corruption, at least two parties are needed! (This author's interpretation of 9/11 is that two centres for US economic and military power were publicly executed by young Wahhabites from Saudi Arabia).
Conflict Worker:	After 11 September the conflict spread. What is the goal?
American:	The goal is *free trade without borders*, globalised, making it possible to meet any demand with a supply everywhere. Freedom means being able to buy and sell whatever, wherever and whenever one wants.
Muslim:	The goal is *respect for our religion*, seeing trade as a deeply human relation far beyond supply meeting demand and products being exchanged for money, in the West even without eye contact!

The solution for 9/11 could have been that world society punishes the perpetrators for their criminal act, and that the USA apologises and withdraws economically and militarily from Saudi Arabia. Unwanted penetration and transformation of somebody else's country is illegitimate.

But the broader conflict between free trade and respect is more problematic. And the conflict is certainly not formulated as a conflict between such constructive goals as free trade and respect:

- What do the parties want? Free trade! Respect!
- What is legitimate and what is illegitimate in these two goals?
- Is it possible to build a bridge between the legitimate parts of the goals?

But instead of this kind of exercise the parties try to realise destructive goals by destruction and murder in Manhattan and Washington on 9/11 and in Afghanistan from 7 October. And the media follow.

The basic diagram has to be extended so that it also includes negative goals.

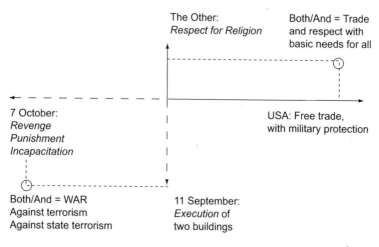

Conflict diagram for 9/11 + 7 October 2001

This could easily last 500 years and how it will all end nobody knows. But we know that journalists and politicians have a tendency to become obsessed with the bottom left quadrant, guided by the two questions of classic *war journalism*: Where is the violence? Who is winning? Bush keeps talking about exterminating evil, and Bin Laden about justice and retaliation.

Let us now add to this a look at the upper right quadrant, with the two questions of *peace journalism*: What is the conflict about? Are there solutions, with acceptable, sustainable outcomes?

If Other realises his goal, we would get isolated groups in Saudi Arabia's desert, perhaps also along the coast, living the life they have been living for centuries, with much emphasis on spiritual values and religious traditions. There are others, like the Amish in Pennsylvania, of that kind. This may be a solution for them, but for the world as a whole it's totally unacceptable, with women oppressed by some of the religions that demand respect.

If the USA should attain its goal, the world would become USA-dominated, a militarily protected (and bombed) shopping mall with single-minded emphasis on material values, on things, property, consumption, and with other cultures at the margins of society and ultimately disappearing. A solution for some, but for the world as a whole totally unacceptable. Free trade *kills* by being unable to satisfy basic needs for food and health at the bottom of world society. And those who are fighting against this are *killed* – by 'military protection'

– for instance, during the first 11 September, in 1973, the intervention and coup in Chile against a democratically elected government.

A compromise could be *globalisation-free zones* where the population is not ready, or willing, to submit itself to global market forces because borderless trade with monetisation and privatisation kills those without resources.

Positive transcendence would celebrate the positive aspects of religion by giving meaning to life, and the positive aspects of trade by increasing our choice of goods, and connecting human beings across borders. The evils of religion and trade are what should be eliminated, and that is best done by placing the satisfaction of human basic needs for survival, well-being, freedom and identity, and basic human rights for all, as the measure of all things, and as the first priority.

CONFLICT PARTIES AND CONFLICT THIEVES: TRANSCENDENCE THROUGH DIALOGUE

Conflict theory is riddled with conflicts over how conflicts are to be handled, over the best, the most valid theory of conflict. And the central conflict is between the inner and the outer, mediating, parties.

The Inner Parties: Conflicts should be handled by us from within, jointly. Only we know exactly what the issue is, and by working together towards a solution we will own not only the conflict but the solution. Together we shall develop ourselves and acquire a sense of shared responsibility. Anybody who is managing this conflict from the outside takes the conflict away from its rightful owners and becomes (in Nils Christie's brilliant formulation) a *conflict thief.*

The Outer Parties: Conflicts have to be managed from without because the internal parties have a too limited perspective. They are not aware that in an ever-shrinking world conflicts are relevant to all of us, even owned by all of us. In addition to that, the internal parties are blinded by their emotions and lack the competence to master the task in their *conflict egotism.*

Both are strong and to some extent valid arguments. There is often a reference to psychotherapy, Carl Rogers' 'non-directive counselling', helping the client to arrive at a diagnosis, prognosis and therapy. Sigmund Freud told his patients what the diagnosis and prognosis were, and prescribed a therapy. The arguments for and against are about the same.

As we proceed through micro–meso–macro–mega, from conflicts within and among human beings to conflicts among regions and civilisations, more conflict power is usually given to the external parties, for instance, in Yugoslavia. More particularly, big powers are often convinced that they have to handle macro- and mega-conflicts. Only they have a sufficient overview, including over their own interests. With secret 'services' sabotaging, provoking, intervening they try to make their assumptions self-fulfilling. Big countries are afraid of all state-nation conflicts over autonomy because any solution can encourage their own minorities. Macro-conflicts will always loosen up the state system somewhat, and big countries try to dominate negotiations in order to get bases, resources, markets, clients, etc. To get a seat at the top table they want violence to continue until the internal parties are 'ripe' (exhausted), on their knees begging for assistance from the external parties.

These are strong arguments in favour of internal party control at the macro-level. And the answer from the outside is predictable: OK, go ahead, you are not going to cope anyway.

Author: Here we have arrived at a central point in the TRANSCEND method. Precisely this conflict between the internal and external parties is what we try to transcend. Both parties have good arguments, so there should be a basis for transcendence. It is easy to sympathise with the internal parties observing how the external parties do not transform, but 'wrongform', the whole conflict to their own advantage. But are the internal parties alone able to transcend and transform?

What is needed for transcendence is creativity within and among the internal parties. If the conditions round the negotiating table are right, and if the parties try to be less hostile to each other, then soft, direct negotiations may produce results. The problem is that strong emotions will tend to make them look to the past rather than to the future, and to emphasise the destructive rather than the constructive. A destructive past orientation, particularly when shared, can paralyse all creativity.

For that reason some external parties who neither 'wrongform' nor steal, are needed. The TRANSCEND method tries to stimulate the creativity of the parties by having dialogue with all of them, starting with one at a time. The result can then be used as material for the next round of dialogues. The conflict worker is playing more roles in the same person. She/he facilitates, tries to make them see each other in a more positive light. But she/he hesitates to put forward proposals they have not arrived at themselves. She/he can stimulate and suggest, but always with a question mark, and never insisting on one's own proposal. The method used is the questioning dialogue, not the proclaiming debate. The art consists in stimulating without taking over the process and ultimately calling a press conference in order to communicate to the world the proposal that untied the knot. The parties first have to meet alone at the 'small table' for dialogue with the mediator in order to be ready to meet round the 'big table' for negotiations.

The parties have positions that contradict each other. Let us call these positions in old, Daoist/dialectical tradition from China, via Matteo Ricci, Leibniz and Hegel to Marx and his successors, *thesis* and *antithesis*. We have seen many in this book. Sometimes they are rather steeply pitted against each other as those two words indicate. But the word *synthesis* is not very useful as it makes no distinction between compromise, positive transcendences and negative transcendences.

The task of the conflict worker is not to stop the dialectic by demanding that the parties abandon their positions, unless they are clearly illegitimate. The task is rather to make them avoid a flat compromise with nothing creative, nothing new, nothing renewing reality. The conflict worker is listening to the dialectic in order, together with the parties, to find a positive transcendence, which builds a bridge between the goals, or a negative transcendence with rejects them both.

The task of a conflict worker is to stimulate the parties to arrive at new ideas and thoughts that empower them to take the leap into a renewing reality where they all can find their place, proud of the fact that they have created it themselves, albeit with some assistance and much encouragement.

In this process the conflict worker puts his own goals openly on the table. The goals are *empathy*, a deep understanding of all parties, their goals and the goals behind the goals; *creativity* and *non-violence*, to arrive at something new that is acceptable and sustainable. For this something old has to be abandoned, even destroyed in that there may be seeds of violence. And for that reason the new should not be so new that it is incomprehensible, even menacing.

This birth process has to be assisted and in a loving way. There is an enormous reservoir of energy in any conflict, which can be used to transform the conflict upwards, towards creativity and non-violence. What has to be avoided is a transformation downwards, to aggression and violence, through the flatness of the compromise or the cowardice of withdrawal, let alone fighting for extremist positions. The conflict worker is the midwife of this process, as Sicily's Gandhi, Danilo Dolci, always emphasised.

GANDHI'S NON-VIOLENCE: RESIST EVIL, PROTECT PEOPLE

Freud personalised conflicts and put them inside us, not as a struggle between God and Satan, but as a struggle between norms and values from the outside, from parents and others, and the drives within us. Only by thoroughly cleansing the history of this struggle, sedimented in our own subconscious, our baggage, can we ever hope to master our personal conflicts.

Marx socialised the conflicts and situated them into the relation between the classes, not in the difference between them. This was not a question of serf and lord learning how to relate to each other as Hegel proposed, but of changing the relation between them. Only by thoroughly cleansing our social deep structure can we ever hope to master our social conflicts.

Mandela and de Klerk focused on the problems created by the violence. Only by thoroughly cleansing the relation between perpetrator and victim, through truth and reconciliation, can we ever hope to master a relation that casts long shadows across the future. They produced an alternative to the Western judicial tradition, in both theory and practice.

Gandhi's lifelong struggle with himself places him in the first chapter of this book, the micro. His struggle against gender repression, racism, caste, exploitation of workers/peasants/villagers, for *sarvodaya* ('uplift'), development, places him in the meso. His struggle for peace and reconciliation between Hindus and Muslims places him in the macro. And his struggle against English/Western imperialism, for self-rule, *swaraj*, places him in the mega. He transcended the contradiction between English colonialism and *swaraj*. Inner 'self-rule' as a compromise was rejected in two ways. One was negative, neither/nor, as village autonomy, *panchayat raj*. The other was positive, both/and, as *rama raj*, his way of saying 'the kingdom of God on earth', for everybody, including the English, but then as friends, not as colonialists.

We now give Gandhi the last conflict in this book, with his non-violence, valid along the whole micro–meso–macro–mega-spectrum, up to the struggle between civilisations.

What was his problem, his 'conflict', dilemma? Thesis: *Gandhi's problem was to protect human beings and at the same time fight the evil in himself, in others, in groups, states, nations, civilisations.* Everything human carries something good and something evil. The simplest would be the dualist perspective of seeing a human being as totally good or totally evil. Or to find some tepid in-between position.

Gandhi's positive transcendence, his non-violence, combines civil disobedience and non-cooperation with the illegitimate *and* at the same time protection of human beings, the legitimate, also adversaries. Example: he refused to cooperate with the English as colonialists but at the same time met them as human beings outside their work, as civilians, as third parties. He boycotted English textiles and at the same time collected money so that the families of the merchants should not suffer. In other words, clear resistance against suppressing and exploiting structures, without any violence that could insult basic human needs, and at the same time positive support for the legitimate needs of the other side as human beings. The human being on the other side should always feel safe. Everything human that is legitimate had a friend in Gandhi.

By using a word like 'evil' we are painting the Other black, his thoughts, words and deeds, societies, states and nations, structures and cultures. We issue a licence for extermination, the gulag, Auschwitz, Hiroshima, to the bombs of the terrorists and state terrorists. By using the word 'good' we are painting ourselves white, even elevating ourselves to the status of gods. Dualism knows only two colours. The West often refers to this attitude as 'realism' and brands Gandhi as an 'idealist', remote from reality. Nevertheless, the kernel of Anglo-Saxon realism was melting in the warmth radiating from Gandhi's combination of struggle and compassion. Who was the realist? Who was out of touch with human reality? He who not only fought colonialism at the same time as he was protecting the colonialists, and saw his own shortcomings and engaged in a lifelong project for self improvement? Or the colonialists, with their punishment expeditions and prison for the 'uppity'?

'Non-violence' expresses this badly. Gandhi used *satyagraha*, clinging to truth. For him Truth, Love and God expressed the same thing. Truth is what you stand up for; Love is how you meet the other party; God is what ties us together in one humanity.

Whether the conflict is with a spouse, another class, another country or another region in the world, violence is to be rejected. If you harm Other then you also harm yourself. We are all parts of the same unity of humanity. In addition, you are aiming in the wrong direction. The problem is not Other. You can incapacitate him so that he is incapable of achieving his evil goals. But this will not solve the contradiction at the deeper level which will survive both him and you. All you have done is to kill a fellow human being, a fellow life.

Christian theology, particularly the Catholic version, makes a beautiful distinction between the sin and the sinner. The sin in thought, word and action is totally rejected. But the sinner can be forgiven and resurrected if he himself rejects his sin and cleanses himself through penitence. 'Look with mercy on me, a poor sinner.' Beautiful, because it clings to a nucleus that can be saved instead of rejecting, killing, exterminating everything through capital punishment, murder, war, terrorism and state terrorism. The Church practises this better than the courts, through *grace*. With life imprisonment, not to mention capital punishment of the sinner, the courts are denying themselves this distinction, except when grace is administered by the head of state, thereby elevating himself to the status of God.

The point is to direct the struggle against the act, the word, perhaps also the thought, but not against the person. Take the ball, not the player. The struggle is against the antagonism, not the antagonist. Against the dictatorship, not against the dictator, the way vulgar democrats do. Against capitalism, not against the capitalist, the way vulgar Marxists do. Against the wrong idea, like 'We are chosen by Yahweh/God/Allah and for that reason are above the law', not against the carrier of that idea, like vulgar terrorists do.

But does this also hold for Hitler, the litmus test of non-violence? The traditional understanding is that Hitler was as a *monster*, evil to the core. A clear candidate for extermination, execution. He also committed suicide in order to deprive others of that opportunity, hardly because he saw himself as evil.

Instead of that perspective, let us look at Hitler as the carrier of a bundle of six extremely bad ideas that found a meeting point in him, like micro-organisms and parasites find their prey:

France has to be taught a lesson; in other words, the pedagogy of punishment, very common in schools when Hitler was a child.

All Germans have to come together in one country; in other words, the nation-state philosophy as developed by such German philosophers as Herder and Fichte.

Germany has the same right to colonies as Spain and Portugal, England and France, the Netherlands and Belgium, etc.

The Slavic peoples, particularly the Russians, are innately inferior and fit for colonisation, as slaves; in other words, the same contempt for the Slavic peoples that can be found in Marx as 'a-historical peoples'.

The Jews are vermin; in other words, the same bottomless hatred that we can find, for instance, in Martin Luther, the father of German Protestantism.

Vermin have to be exterminated; in other words, the same chemical attitude to life that can be found in Bayer AG toward micro-organisms (the sulphur pharmaceuticals as antibiotics).

Four of these six ideas are German. In Hitler the Germans met themselves on the threshold.

Exterminate Hitler and the ideas will, like micro-organisms, start searching for new hosts. The defence against extreme violence lies in the immune system against such ideas. But the German-Austrian collective deep culture surrounding Hitler was an excellent breeding ground. How do we strengthen human beings against such things? How do we build an immune system against such ideas? By strengthening cultural peace and deep cultural peace. At the beginning of the 1930s this would imply massive resistance against Nazi extermination ideas and against extreme violence, non-cooperation and at the same time direct dialogue. Massive economic boycott, and at the same time assistance and support to those who are suffering. But such indications are a part of the theory of peace. Let us continue exploring Gandhi's theory of conflict.

Gandhi transcended the contradiction between liberals who are against direct violence but not against structural exploitation, and Marxists who are against structural exploitation but not against revolutionary violence. Gandhi was fighting violence and exploitation, as evil deeds, evil structures and evil cultures, and protected human beings against both of them through his *sarvodaya*.

If what ties us together in one humanity is God, then God's message also has to have a certain unity. The True nucleus is that God is the same as Love. This is incompatible with a punitive God who communicates in one language to His chosen people, and excludes all others who are not seeking Him through that one teaching. To Gandhi an excluding God is false. He celebrates an including God by reading from the Bible, the Qu'ran, the Bhagavad-Gita, always choosing soft, non-violent texts, on countless occasions. For the linguistically very competent Gandhi the thesis that God is the same as Truth and Love, and for that reason makes himself comprehensible to all human beings in all cultures, must have been a truism. With his rich, beautiful English and his perfect Sanskrit, Hindi/Urdu and Gujarati, he was very well fitted for the giant task celebrated here: Gandhi's *ecumenism*. The unity of life, the unity of humanity, has to find its counterpart in the unity of the message so that human beings across all conflict divides can see each other as sacred and dignified, and direct the struggle where it should be directed.

Gandhi's transcendence of the hard, excluding religions' either/ or, in favour of an including both/and of the softer aspects, went beyond the usual come-together of Protestantisms, Christianities or Abrahamitic religions best known in the West as the ecumenical movement. The proposition 'God is inside us' and 'We are all in God' must have been synonymous for Gandhi, thereby transcending the contradiction between an immanent and transcendent concept of God. Gandhi was *poly-religious* not only *polyglot*; a more organic, positive transcendence than to try to arrive at an Esperanto of all religions, a common denominator. His dividing line was not between religions, but between the hard and the soft aspects in all of them. *Thank you*, Gandhi.

Friday: Deep Culture,
Deep Behaviour, Deep Structure

We often have the feeling that there is something beneath the surface, or behind.

A party to a conflict, at any level, who says something about a conflict is producing a 'text'. It has been enormously helpful for the social sciences and history to learn from the science of literature how to do textual analysis. Thus, we can introduce silent *undertexts*, *overtexts* and *contexts* to understand better what has been said in the original text. We read about the significance of helping Albanians in Kosovo/a for humanitarian reasons, but at the same time there is a covert undertext about the significance of having military bases in that area and of securing oil pipelines from the Caspian region to the Adriatic. Elsewhere there is an unmentioned overtext about the significance of giving NATO a new role and of being loyal to NATO and the USA. And there is a larger geopolitical context where control over Eurasia is fundamental.

To be honest is to verbalise together the under-, over- and contexts with the texts. In the long term honesty may be more sustainable, but we can be certain that honesty will take a long time. In addition, the state system elevates dishonesty to 'statecraft'. If a text delivered by a foreign minister coincides with reality, then it must be purely coincidental because texts today are written by 'spin-doctors' in order to produce an acceptable image of reality, not to reflect what is really going on.

But this is the trivial aspect of 'there is something underneath', the consciously manipulated. We are more interested in the subconscious, in the *deep texts,* which drive the parties without them being fully aware of what is happening, because it has been suppressed, because it has become a habit, or simply because it looks so obviously an expression of what is normal and natural that it remains unarticulated.

In this book we have been exploring three components in a conflict: *attitude, behaviour and contradiction* – ABC. What we are now saying is that in addition to ABC there are deep attitudes, deep behaviour and deep contradictions. As a rule these are not verbalised. They are this 'something underneath' and are absolutely crucial if we are to understand a conflict and do a good job at transcendence and transformation. For that reason we have to get closer, perhaps by giving them another name.

An attitude can usually be written as a rule, a prescription for how to act in certain situations, which are then described. Kant was of the opinion that such rules should be 'universalisable', in other words, they are not something valid only for you, in the here and now, but for everybody in the same situation. You can follow Kant at this point by writing down the rule that expresses your action, looking at it and see whether you can accept it as a general rule, as a 'maxim'. Not a bad idea.

What then is this 'something underneath', Kant's position? Why do rules have to be universalisable? Imagine that humanity is divided into civilisations, which are in turn divided into cultures, and that all of them view many things in their own way. In some cultures, for instance, life is more sacred than in others. Imagine that Kant is of the opinion that whoever takes the life of another does not have the right to his own, in other words, he will suffer capital punishment, and justifies this position by universalisability. To his own civilisation, yes, perhaps – German, Christian, Occidental. But to a Buddhist culture in an Oriental civilisation definitely no. Perhaps Kant himself was also an unreflected spokesperson for Occidental deep culture and its obsession with universalisation, seeing everything Western as universal and the West as the driving force of humanity, and for that reason was universalising universalisation itself? In other words, beware.

DEEP CULTURE

The two giants in understanding human beings, Sigmund Freud and Carl Jung, recognised a division of labour. Freud saw deep attitudes beneath the attitudes in the individual; Jung saw deep attitudes beneath the attitudes in collectivities. Both saw both. Jung's work with the 'shadow' – the attitudes we do not acknowledge that we have – and Freud's work on monotheism, are good examples. Let us call these deep attitudes the *individual subconscious* and the *collective subconscious*. There is nothing mysterious about the 'collective', it refers only to deep attitudes which members of a certain category appear to share. The assumption is that similar impressions have shaped them in more or less the same way, exposed to the same impressions. There is no assumption of a 'collective soul' or anything of that kind. Let us use the expression *deep culture* about the collective subconscious, which the culture quite often does not recognise.

This, however, is becoming too abstract. Our task is to show that deep culture has a role to play and is important in shaping attitudes and behaviour in a conflict. In other words, *conflict culture* has to be included in conflict work. As an example, let us compare autonomy conflicts involving three nations with different conflict cultures in the Iberian peninsula: Castile centred on Madrid, Catalonia centred on Barcelona, and Euskadi = the Basque Country. The conflicts are the autonomy/independence conflict between Catalonia and Castile, and the autonomy/independence conflict between Euskadi and Castile.

Our concern is the impact of deep culture on conflict culture. If, for instance, deep culture has already taken a stand, even a strong stand, on which of the five outcomes in a conflict over two incompatible goals is/are preferred/privileged, then that is certainly of basic significance for prognosis and therapy.

The parties will be driven towards that or those outcome(s) even without being conscious of what is happening because it is already stored in the subconscious, and without any protest because that subconsciousness is shared by all or most of them.

As the two conflicts have Castile in common, let us start there, with Castilian deep culture.

The thesis is that the deep culture of Castile will privilege two extremist positions with a winner and a loser, and is weak on withdrawal, compromise and transcendence (the peace diagonal).

That does not necessarily imply violence, even though that particular conflict culture is compatible with violence. We are dealing with a typical, aristocratic, deep culture with roots in the feudal Middle Ages, exemplified by duels and tournaments and battles. It is not unique to Castilian Spain, but figures in many parts of Europe.

But there are other ways of dominating (*dominus* = lord) than by the *sword*. One method is to enact the conflict verbally, using a *court* as the arena since juridical deep culture also privileges extremist positions ('A is guilty, B is innocent'); with a small escape valve for withdrawal: 'the case is dismissed'.

A third approach is to use money, purchasing victory; this is also known as *corruption*. Yet another way of appointing a winner is through a *vote* where simple arithmetic liberates the parties from the laborious task of finding a compromise or a transcendence, keeping 'the decision is deferred' as a withdrawal possibility.

And then yet another factor, which is very important in Castile: *charisma*, power rooted in the radiation of a personality, often upgrading that person to a *Don* (Don Juan is indicative of a special type of radiation). The Don enters a room. He is met with respectful silence. Seated at the table, people present their views. Slowly all attention focuses on him. He is the last speaker, his is the last word, the summary, the conclusion. Many Dons live in Madrid.

Regardless of the method or mechanism used, the conflict is decided by determining who the winner is.

Where does this come from? Perhaps we can even talk about a deep culture, a basement beneath the basement, with a strong bonding to the number '2', and a strong faith that God/Justice is talking with a clear voice through the outcome. That divine clarity will disappear in the paleness of compromise, the cowardice of withdrawal and the human creativity of any transcendence.

If God had wanted transcendence, He would not have given His Spanish subjects so many forms of confrontation. He would have shown that transcendence in His act of Creation. Instead, he gave the Spanish the ability to express His will by winning in various ways.

But do the Spanish believe this today? They may be doing so unconsciously because the basement beneath the basement is even less accessible. Faith in '2' (outcomes) may outlive faith in God and be carried by faith in Justice. *'Plus ça change, plus c'est la même chose'*, the French say – 'The more things change, the more they stay the same.' The rat '2' deserting the sinking ship of aristocratic duels of long ago did not jump into the water in order to drown, but to find another ship. And that same rat has been living in courtrooms for some time now. Hence the very apt expression a 'court duel'.

But there is another, powerful carrier of this deep culture in Spain: the *corrida*, the bullfight, with two actors, *Toro* (the bull) and *Matador* (the killer) and two outcomes. Matador kills almost always and Toro is sent to the butcher. Very rarely Toro gets Matador on the horns and Matador is taken to the hospital.

Toro and Matador going on strike, sitting down, one eating, the other smoking grass, is certainly withdrawal, but would be defined as cowardice. Compromise, fight only until Toro is wounded, may be good enough for sissies, wimps, like the French and the Portuguese.

Transcendence as a suicide pact, Toro and Matador running in parallel, against each other, is morbid. Negative transcendence in the sense of Toro and Matador running together, attacking the judge, or the public, is interesting, but hardly realistic, however. A heretic proposal only, from a Norwegian observer?

A bullfight is like a text, and one deep text has already been indicated: a conflict has two and only two outcomes. This is normal, natural. Life is like that and will stay that way.

But there is another and very compatible deep text.

Toro has a highly visible and frequently mentioned part, the *cojones*, the testicles. Likewise, Matador has tight silk trousers which leave no doubt that he also has something between his legs. Reading: this 'either-you-or-me' fight is between men. Real men.

Some years ago a very skilful female bullfighter appeared, literally, in the bullring, a clear transgression of that deep culture. She was harassed away fairly quickly. Had she focused on cow fighting, the boys might have acquiesced, even with pleasure. She would have found her place.

Then there is a third deep text: Toro is raw, brutal nature; black, the colour of darkness, from the deeper crevices of reality, Satan's colour. Matador is not only a man but is handsome, attractive; he is force, skill, technique, style. He is dancing an aesthetic ballet of death around Toro. Not just man against brute, but culture against nature are being celebrated in this fatal conflict culture.

Then there is Catalonia. They are citizens of the same Spanish state, but have a very different deep culture where conflict is concerned. Compromise is privileged, the reasonable outcome, a place in the middle for reasonable parties. The carriers of this deep culture are even more important than bullfights: merchants, buying and selling, bargaining, negotiating in the market to obtain the best – meaning acceptable and sustainable – possible bargain. Ideally, this takes place without coercion or threats, making both sides feel like winners, avoiding any glory/trauma mentalities. Temporary withdrawal from the process is possible. Whatever the outcome let common sense (Catalan: *seny*) prevail.

But there is no transcendence. What is negotiated to find a compromise is defined by the parties and their positions. And that dimension should be divisible so that jumping and sliding up and down is possible. The price, in freshly minted coins, is ideal for that purpose.

The alternative is horse trading between two goals, exchanging something indivisible for something else that is also indivisible.

This characterises an entire nation. The compromise of the merchants is as normal and natural as the warfare of the aristocrats.

Consciousness is low in either case, except when they are confronted with the conflict style of the other party. Even Madrid has to negotiate. Perhaps Madrid feels more at ease with the more belligerent Basques?

Are these stereotypes? To some extent, yes. But they cannot be disproved by public opinion polls tapping only the conscious. We are in the field of cultural anthropology, a component of interdisciplinary conflict studies. The method is observation, participation, empathy. Above all careful, probing dialogues to gain insight into how conflict parties experience conflicts, deep down.

Then, there are the Basques. One simple formulation: Castile *in extremis*, more Spanish than the Spaniards themselves. Ignatius Loyola and his *Compañia de Jesús* (the Jesuits) were more Catholic than the pope. Pit them against Castile and the result is given in advance: two parallel bullfights. Their heavy common history is the history of the struggle to win. Franco's España, *una, grande, libre*, implied bloody suppression of the Basques. Their answer was to counter Franco's regime with car bombs, ultimately gaining some autonomy, but not the independence ETA wants. The car bombs continued. The socialist government responded by killing, using secret police. The conservatives responded with polarisation, isolation. Two ETA leaders got more than 1,000 years in prison. And a political party has been banned.

This is a culture of fighting, with violence, polarisation and dichotomies, and goals like 'independence' and 'within the limits of the Spanish Constitution' (meaning the *status quo*). There are no alternatives. The parties are tied to the two extremist outcomes. Withdrawal is cowardice. Compromise is treason. And transcendence demands not only creativity, but also a willingness to see something valid in the other, and that is blocked by the powerful grip deep culture has on conflict culture. People who know little about conflict often believe that a shared culture will bind them together, but that depends on the culture. If violence is lurking beneath the surface, then violence committed by one is confirmation of dualism to the other, and they will live very unhappily together. Forever?

Let's hope not. But the road to a more positive handling of the conflict passes through the painful process of deep culture awareness. There has to be some awareness of the deeper dynamics steering collectivities, taking negative aspects of the collective subconscious so to speak by the throat, throwing it out. Needless to say, that goes for both sides, and probably for men more than for women, and for people in the centre more than for those on the periphery.

At the same time, Catalonia is sliding towards higher levels of autonomy with its two steps forward, one step back. The politician presiding over this process, Pujol, evades the perennial question put by journalists, 'Is the goal independence?' He cannot say 'Yes' without entering the dualist conflict culture, and he cannot say 'No' without surrendering an important bargaining chip. Withdrawal from that conflict is clever.

Between the Basque Country and Catalonia, high up in the Pyrenees, there is a tiny country, Andorra, which for centuries was ruled by an unlikely duo: the King/President of France, and the Bishop of Seo de Urgel, a small town in Spain. Today, the country is an independent member of the United Nations. The culture? Catalan, of course. Small steps. No bombs. One model among several for the Basques? Judging by the outcome, the answer is an unqualified yes, but as a method more problematic. All that peaceful negotiation, renouncing a clear victory, triumphantly marching into San Sebastian (Donostia) at the end, is very much at variance with a deep culture also expressing itself with bombs.

One country, three nations, at least. The Tortoise Catalonia will arrive at high autonomy before a culture-trapped Achilles Basque. It's difficult to speculate so far into the future, but it could harbour a Madrid facing a Barcelona not its equal but its superior because Madrid remains trapped in a stupid double bullfight with the Basque Country. Ideas of national autonomy never seem to die. Leaders may be killed, movements may be crushed, but the idea of being ruled by one's own kind will survive, strongly anchored in the deep culture of any nation.

Let us take another example, this time more geopolitical. Conflict culture is certainly important, and even more so the deep culture in the basement. In the deep culture = collective subconscious Jung's archetypes are like atoms of subconscious meaning, an example being the 'twoness' frequently referred to above. Archetypes may combine into molecules of higher complexity, 'syndromes', and 'super-syndromes' –more like protein molecules, to stick to the molecule metaphor.

One such syndrome is the strong belief in being a Chosen People (C), with a Glorious past and/or future (G), at the same time suffering from countless Trauma (T). This adds up to the CGT syndrome, among the most problematic in macro- and mega-conflicts. At the level of the individual this would be a person with a mandate from God, with glory expected in the future, but also deeply marked and marred by trauma, real or imagined, inflicted by others. There is a certain inner logic to this. He who has God's mark on his forehead is predestined to greatness, but he will also inspire enormous envy, and others will want to get him.

At the personal micro-level such a person suffers from megalomania, paranoia and will be psychiatrised under the rubric of narcissism/paranoia. But at the state macro-level this national pathology is still sometimes classified as patriotism, love of the fatherland, and is much celebrated.

As deep culture this confronts us with enormous problems. A state driven by a dominant nation with this kind of baggage in its deep culture has an enormous incentive to subjugate others, a major factor dividing Western colonialism. But how will such chosen nations relate to each other?

Let us look at four cases (see table).

	USA	Israel	Iraq	Serbia
Chosen	by God	by Yahweh	by Allah	by Bog = God
Glory	after the Second World War	Israel I David	Sumer, Babylon	28/6/1914
		Israel II 1947–?	Abassides	Yugoslavia
Trauma	Vietnam 11/9/2001	Shoah	Baghdad 1258 Colonialism	28/6/1389 28/6/2001

The God of the Western and Eastern Churches, the Yahweh of Judaism and the Allah of Islam – the Abrahamitic trinity – all have their Chosen Peoples. They have their glory from the past and their deep trauma. The table can be challenged, but the syndromes clearly have some similarities. All four states/nations base their legitimacy on a God with universal pretensions. But there is an important difference: the USA sees itself as universally valid, but the same cannot be said about Israel, Iraq and Serbia. They may be regional powers, but the USA is a world power, even a world model in its own eyes and those of many others.

So they are on a collision course. Hitler saw his people as chosen by 'Providence' and richly equipped with glory and trauma. The collision course with the Jews was on the cards for a long time, especially after the strongly anti-Semitic Martin Luther gave the Christian God a more German profile. That the USA is not on a collision course with Israel is related to the strong position of the Jews in the USA since the 1950s. If the Iraqis and the Serbs had been able to secure a similar position in the USA both the Gulf and the Yugoslav wars would have been inconceivable. Both nations would have had solid representatives in the State Department. We know how it was and what happened. We also sense one of the roots of the super-tension between Israel and Iraq. They have the same problem as Serbia. The problem is not an Ariel Sharon, a Saddam Hussein or a Slobodan Milosevic, but a pathological deep culture, which may survive all of these characters.

Of course, more can be said and the reader will find more in *Peace by Peaceful Means,* Part IV, Civilization Theory. Thus, there is something about the differences in space and time perspectives among civilisations. The USA, the Occident *in extremis*, has an unlimited space perspective, which includes not only Planet Earth but the whole universe. But the time perspective is limited, like 'before Thanksgiving/Christmas' or 'within this Administration'. Serbia is the contrast. Bog, the Orthodox God, gave them a mission as bulwark against the Muslim/Ottoman advance, stationed in small territories in Kosovo/a, Bosnia and Croatia. The Christianity they had been chosen to protect turned against them, however, hated and exterminated them, 'out of envy'. But Serbia, backed by God, will rise from the ashes, again and again, after defeat and retreat; perennial themes in the Serbian passion story. *Defeat, retreat, return.*

Iraq has a similar extended time perspective, including the defeat of Babylon and the Abassides; the massacre of Baghdad in 1258 by the Mongols, backed by the pope; the Ottoman Empire; the 1916 treason by Sykes/Picot (the English and French foreign ministers who promised the Arabs freedom if they fought the Turks, and then colonised them); the province Kuwait that was taken from them in 1898; and the Gulf wars. And yet Iraq has persevered, and will continue to do so. Washington is very impatient with them both. But the one with the longer time perspective will win – in the longer run.

In addition, there is a factor located in Iraq's Bedouin culture. War is not only a question of winning, of obtaining goals 'by all necessary means', preventing the enemy from stopping this happening. That is modern war, Clausewitz's war, the so-called continuation of diplomacy by other means. Victory over Iraq in 1991 was celebrated in the USA because Kuwait was no longer occupied, but liberated from Iraq. The interesting point is that the result of the war was also celebrated by Iraq in February 1991. But can both sides be victorious? Of course they can, if they are fighting two different wars, defined within two different cultures. The USA and the US-led coalition fought a modern war and won. Iraq fought a traditional war rooted in Bedouin deep culture, and Iraqi deep culture in particular. They also won, because in addition to military victory they had three other perspectives: war as a way of displaying *courage*, as a way of obtaining *honour* and *dignity*. If you win militarily, fine – but if you don't, you may still have the other three.

The more allies on the other side, the more soldiers, the more forceful weapons, the better. The more superior the other side, the more courage can be displayed, and honour and dignity harvested. Sooner or later capitulation is necessary in order not to be exterminated. But in the meantime a moral victory has been won, against the naïve 'realist' balance of power theories that superior destructive power should deter, not attract. It's an example of where universalisation with no sense of deep cultural variations may bring us.

If the Iraqis are a chosen people, maybe more by the Arab nation than by Allah, has a very long time perspective, and can harvest traditional victory in spite of modern defeat, then that people are not easily handled by those with the opposite profile. The soldiers of (post)modern warfare are cowards, killing defenceless civilians in Iraq, Serbia and Afghanistan from a height of 14,000 feet. They win, but harvest little honour and still less dignity. Who will win in the longer run?

More can be said. As an explanatory basis for conflict behaviour deep culture is necessary, but not sufficient, only one factor among many.

One more syndrome: DMA, Dualism, Manicheism, Armageddon.

A short version of the Bible and the Abrahamitic religions: There are two forces in the world, Good and Evil, represented by God and Satan, and irreconcilable controversies must end in a final battle, Armageddon. Conclusion from the point of view of conflict culture: withdrawal, compromise and peaceful transcendence are all meaningless. That battle is itself the transcendence. A very poor conflict menu served by those religions.

'Irreconcilable' means 'you or me'. The decision mechanism is in the violence; not in a court case, corruption, voting or charisma. Fundamentalists in all three religions, and their secular successors, will block all efforts to expand the conflict culture to include the peace diagonal. They seek violence.

But the DMA syndrome has other and equally destructive consequences.

Polarisation in two blocs, with only good to say about themselves and only evil to attribute to each other, is common when a conflict is protracted and is over such important goals as basic needs. But the one suffering from the DMA syndrome is already pre-polarised. All he needs is a good enemy so they can complement each other. They understand each other by reading themselves.

Polarisation facilitates the exercise of violence because DMA has already dehumanised Other. Polarisation also makes it easier to suffer violence. Violence committed by Evil is a confirmation of one's own goodness even if violence is humiliating and expresses contempt. DMA also blocks any real understanding of Other. If Other is Evil, then why try to understand his goals? Better to reveal his evil nature; don't give him a voice, a face. If that makes him desperate and violent, this only proves what we already know: he *is* evil. Who wants to know Serbia's goals in the conflict in and around Yugoslavia when Serbia simply is evil? Or Jakarta's worries in connection with East Timor? Such knowledge is effectively eradicated by the DMA syndrome. A vicious and very problematic cycle.

DEEP BEHAVIOUR

This is behaviour in latent form, somewhere deep down, working its way to the surface. We shall identify it with action emanating from basic needs. An example: dialogue with a leading Soviet functionary in the 1970s about military doctrines. After a good conversation I noticed that he was looking at a watch, not his own in order to check the time, but mine. After a bit he was unable to suppress the question he wanted to ask: where had I bought the watch, and how much did it cost? The watch was digital, something new at the time. The need that verbal action came out of had something to do with identity, with what was fashionable at the time, in the West. What filled the heart, the mouth, had, sooner or later, to be articulated.

The point is that deep behaviour influences surface actions and sometimes distorts them. Thus, diplomats may be offered gifts – luxury meals, call girls – in the hope that this will influence their behaviour at the negotiating table towards a Yes. If they are tired of luxury meals, but not of sex, the verbal behaviour may easily become a Yes.

A 'peace treaty' that suppresses basic needs such as identity, freedom and well-being is an anti-peace treaty. Deep behaviour will force its way into the daylight, like seeds under asphalt, and burst mountains like freezing water in the crevices. In saying so we are not saying that violence itself is a basic need. If that was the case, we would have had much more violence, which is not as easily explained in terms of blocked basic needs, deep culture and deep structure.

The violence will be directed against whatever is blocking basic needs, but can also be displaced in any direction. If violence is the smoke, then the fire is blocked basic needs. One of them is identity, and a part of identity is to have control over one's own situation. But if the conflict is with a big power or a majority suffering from DMA, then he will not understand because he is not going to listen. DMA produces violence because polarisation makes a person deaf. Dialogue is badly needed if a peaceful solution is to be found.

Basic rule: *Audiatur et altera pars*, listen to all parties. Respect them. Give them a voice. Transcendence may be just around the corner (see the dialogue with the Indonesian general, Saturday).

DEEP STRUCTURE

Deep contradictions are located in the deep structure. That makes us call on another master with roots in the nineteenth century: Karl Marx. He used contradictions to understand the structure, particularly class, more particularly economic class, and even more specifically the contradiction between those who own, and those who do not own, means of production and for that reason are astride the fulcrum of history.

Let's expand that perspective and look at some other deep contradictions – deep in the sense that we can talk about 'tectonic' plates producing social earthquakes, not only within a society of persons, but also within a world society of states (see table).

All these deep contradictions are vertical, between high and low, and they are all potential carriers of structural violence. But can we say that states are gendered? If we use a brutal formulation like the contradiction between 'to take' and 'to be taken', then yes. And the USA tries to label deviant states using the concept of 'rogue state', an expression which is now being applied to itself.

	At the level of persons	*At the level of states*
Relative to nature	Waste, throw away, kill	Waste, throw away, kill
Between genders	Take and be taken	Take and be taken
Between generations	Oldest, middle, youngest	Oldest, middle, youngest
Between races	White, coloured	White, coloured
Between classes	Powerful-powerless	Powerful–Powerless
• political	Decision power	Decision power
• military	Coercion power	Coercion power
• economic	Reward power	Reward power
• cultural	Persuasion power	Persuasion power
Relative to deviance	Normal–Deviant	Normal–Deviant
	Somatically ill	Somatically ill
	Mentally ill	Mentally ill
	Criminal	Criminal
Between nations and civilisations	West–Rest	West–Rest
Relative to countries, territorially	Centre–Periphery, within and between states	Centre–Periphery, within and between regions

Conflicts can, ought to, must be understood against the background of the contradictions in the deep structure. Freud, for instance, was studying hysterical women who had enormous difficulties with themselves and their surroundings, and psychologised them in his well-known manner, hunting for the deep structure of the soul. He did not see the deep social structure. Girls could be educated until they were in their early teens; after that they had to be seated and embroider till their hearts were full, in the hope of finding a suitor. But the brother, often less gifted, could continue his studies. His sister might steal into his room to read his books when their parents were asleep. Blocking this need for identity through knowledge would have led to violence among men; with women, violence was directed against themselves. Freud referred to it as 'hysteria'.

Norway, with solid knowledge of and friendship with Serbia after the Second World War, and Spain, with neither knowledge nor friendship, suddenly found themselves on a collision course with Serbia. Spain was bombing the country, Norway was supportive, cowardly. The arguments were hardly convincing even to the governments themselves. But facts were suppressed, DMA and elements of CGT were mobilised to legitimise killing the Serbs. The deep world structure and the deep world culture had both been at work distorting the action: Norway and Spain were both obedient periphery countries in NATO; and in the EU, Spain by being on the inside, the government of Norway by wanting to be on the inside. Consciousness was conditioned by this structural belongingness, and for that reason false in the relationship to Serbia. The governments of both countries had learnt that to be good members of NATO and the EU readiness to kill the Serbs had to be on the agenda. To decide what to do they looked to Washington and Brussels, not Serbia.

Some might find these words hard to take. Not at all, it's only a realistic analysis of what actually happened and is still happening. That doesn't mean that the foreign policy leaders of countries must cancel their memberships and aspirations in order to change policies. But they would need very strong arguments and solidary support from other members to do so. For this political courage – a very scarce commodity in the periphery – is required.

And then there is the gender deep structure. In 1994, I was mediator between Kurdish factions in Rambouillet outside Paris. Their problem was not that Kurdish women dressed in black, marching non-violently on Ankara, would not have a very strong impact. That was precisely the problem, for 'What is going to happen to us men? Women will take over!' Better continue in the old macho ways. Patriarchy without freedom is better than freedom and gender parity?

Deep culture and deep structure can be changed through processes that usually require a lot of time. But deep behaviour derives from basic needs that cannot be changed unless humans undergo genetic manipulation. Why then worry about this when there is nothing we can do about it?

That question is based on a misunderstanding. It is not necessary to change the force of gravity in order to make use of it to our advantage, for instance to give birth or for downhill skiing. The basic point is to understand the force, not to eliminate it, just as it's a good idea to know where the reefs are in order to avoid being stranded. Freedom is insight in necessity, as many philosophers have pointed out. Against such forces, maybe, but real freedom is insight in sufficiency, in what is sufficient to change those forces.

As the parties in a conflict in general are not conscious about the deeper aspects of their own situation, and particularly not about their own cultures, they are badly in need of the conflict worker's charts on which the reefs are supposed to be marked. It's the task of the conflict worker to try, based on what these parties are saying and on taking them seriously, with respect, to make them more aware of what is located beneath the surface. If we ask how the dialogue partners look at conflicts in general, we often get very clear, and sometimes too clear, answers. 'If we don't reach a compromise, there will be a war' – in other words, invoking only the three points on the war diagonal. No lecture will make much of an impression. But good examples from that person's own culture of other ways in which things can be done often have some influence. It's as well to know them.

It is also a good idea to increase their consciousness about their own needs, in order to use them to increase respect for the needs of the other party. 'Don't you think this is as important for those on the other side as it is for you?' is a useful question in a dialogue. It often serves as an eye-opener, leading to an eloquent, acquiescing silence.

Saturday: Creativity, Dialogue, Negotiation

CREATIVITY

Creativity is located in the borderland between the intellectual and the emotional. Knowledge and emotions push together and suddenly there is transcendence, just as it happens to creative people in the arts. The word 'arts' is important here, and is very apt. A good idea starts like an emotion in the guts aching for release, working itself up, arriving in the head/brain where it is verbalised and sent back again to the gut/brain producing a feeling of orgasmic release. Like true love it doesn't happen very often. But when it happens it is overwhelming.

Emotions are the driving forces; intellectuality is the instrument. This apparent contradiction is transcended in conflict work through a passionate rooting in values such as *empathy* to know the parties thoroughly, *creativity* in order to be of any real help, and *non-violence* that promotes, never insults – the basic needs. Conflict work has to be rooted in those values that in turn are put on the table. The non-passionate conflict worker will not do a good job. The motivation is too weak. Mediation is not a job for lukewarm people.

Take a look at the 40 proposals in this book for transcendence and transformation. They are there, in print, before your eyes. They may appear to be trivial. Where is the creativity in this? you may ask. Well, that element was not there when the work was started. At some point that famous leap into the unknown and the unusual has taken place.

At no point do we content ourselves by saying what so many say, 'The parties have to come together.' That is as easily said, and as meaningless, as to say to a person in distress 'Pull yourself together.' Inside all of them there will be a big question: Why? What's the point? We have tried that already, and it didn't help! This is where the conflict worker is needed to point out that little flicker of light at the end of the tunnel, which can ignite a sense of hope.

The person told to 'pull himself together' knows this. The problem is how, where, when, with whom, against whom, and what will make me believe that it will work this time? Someone who has fallen into a river and doesn't know how to swim does not need to be told that he needs to learn how. In order to help you have to know what is needed and contribute something that gives reason for hope in the circumstances.

'What is missing is political will' is another bad formula; it exists at the same low level as 'What is missing is mutual confidence.' Of course they are short on all of this, not because they are genetically incapable of good will and confidence, but because the conflict makes these excellent qualities insufficient. What is missing is almost always 'good ideas'. That is the sticking point.

But there are also situations where even the best ideas will be of no avail. One of the parties simply does not want it, has no will, because he still thinks he can win. He has to be convinced that his victory may come at too great a cost and lead him into a situation where sooner or later he will prefer transcendence that also gives the other party much of what he wants. The American-inspired 'win, win' expresses this badly because it doesn't point to the jump in the transcendence and to a qualitatively new reality. The term is not serious.

The proposals in this book are efforts to be creative without being too creative. The proposals have to be relevant to the conflict as the parties understand it. They have to recognise their own reality. What is new has to be present in the old, and the old present in the new. Sometimes the proposals are simply a list of what we can read out of the peace diagonal without any particular difficulty. But very often there is an element of surprise under the wrappings, something more than the sum of the three points.

Is it possible to learn to be creative? To a certain point, yes. What can be learnt is something everybody can do, and what everybody can do is joint property and hardly deserves the epithet 'creative'. There is something extra on top, some arrow pointing to the future. That ability comes with experience. The first hundred cases are the most difficult.

Don't mystify creativity. Creativity is a jump. But there are also springboards:

(1) *'This reminds me of ...'* Memory is based on personal experience and that of others. There are two ways of being 'reminded': as *identity* and as *isomorphism*, structural identity.

A carpenter has fitted a wardrobe against a wall many times; he then projects his experience into a conflict over where the wardrobe is supposed to go. Answer: this is an identical case, fit it against the wall. A nation wants a high level of autonomy, even independence from the state it sees as its prison, and searches through history and geography to find something similar. In this case there is a considerable probability that he who seeks will also find. But there will always be some objections: this is not at all identical, this is something different. 'There is no comparison' is a strange expression used by many when what they have just done is precisely a comparison, but with the conclusion that the cases are not identical. Nevertheless, the objection has to be taken seriously. What is different and what is similar have to be identified; what this means when the example is used as a model to be drawn upon has to be critically explored.

Thus, a commonly employed objection to a Nordic model in other parts of the world is 'No doubt this works well for you in the North, you are so peaceful.' A short course in Nordic military history will settle that objection. But two points remain: (a) to arrive at this model, hard work is needed; and (b) a solid Nordic civil society. If something is to be used as a model, then all relevant characteristics have to be included. 'You have similar languages.' Well, try that one on the Finnish, the Icelandic, the Sami. Try it on Switzerland. Try the peace-creating potential of same or similar languages, a popular thesis among those who know very little, on the American Civil War. Or on the First and Second World Wars.

Identity can function well only within one of the four levels, whereas isomorphism, structural identity, can be used between the levels. The identity is not in the parties, but in their relationship to each other. Not A = X and B = Y, but A:B = X:Y – A to B like X to Y.

Two countries are solving their border conflict by defining a joint, bi-national zone. In principle, two neighbours can do the same with their gardens. Isomorphism, structural identity, works in space. But does it also work over time? The neighbours will have successors, they don't live forever. Those who acquire the joint property may not themselves have experienced the joy of conflict transformation. Or there may be sellers and buyers who want 'clear boundaries' without constraints on the sale of the plot.

Then maybe the two countries are astute enough nevertheless to draw a border: 'We have found a joint solution, maybe we should in addition, as a fallback position, have a separate solution.' States also have successors, an important problem in international law. But even if the states should be very sustainable, governments may have a shorter life span than an average landowner, and may also find reasons not to be tied by an agreement. Hence, it's as well to think it through.

Here we see the great strength in this method: switching back and forth between A,B and X,Y yields many ideas, not only about what can be done, but also about the problems that might arise. For that reason it is always well to check a good idea at another conflict level. What would this mean if the problem were not between classes in society, but between regions in world society, or between husband and wife? Is there something we should look out for that we are unaware of?

Heuristics is the word for this, a method producing ideas. Isomorphism is even better than identity, precisely because we may be a level or two or three away from the point of departure and there may be more dissimilarities to reflect on. Again, we would claim that this is something everybody can do once they have got the knack.

'Common' people do this kind of thing all the time. Somebody says the same as the conflict worker, 'Could we try what they did in ...' and gets in reply 'But isn't that quite different because ...?'

Now a dialogue is underway. Nothing could be better. They can discuss the conflict as it is in Chinese theatre, by mirroring it in some other conflict.

(2) *Combine known elements in a new way*. There is nothing wrong in challenging, even demanding from parties to an armed conflict that they should have a cease-fire, negotiation and a vision about how to handle the conflict. What works badly, however, is taking these three elements in exactly that order. There are good reasons to believe that the vision comes first, then negotiations after they have 'felt each other's teeth', and finally a cease-fire combined with some extraction of teeth, by which we mean destruction or surrender of arms. In other words, do it in reverse order. Or still better: do all three in parallel, at the same time.

But are they supposed to bring the arms into the negotiation table? Yes, they can do that. The author was once teaching methodology at the University of Havana and was astonished when the students arrived carrying machine guns, which they did not put but threw on the table. They had come straight from military training exercises. It's surprising how quickly one gets used to things like this. It is considerably worse if they come to the table without ideas. Better to bring both arms and ideas than neither one nor the other.

There is much historical tradition and not that much common sense in choosing the order given above, starting with talks about a cease-fire, as the major powers and the United Nations usually do. As mentioned, why should anybody 'decommission' weapons which they think could bring them a military solution, or at least give them defeat with honour if they don't see any light at the end of the tunnel, no transformation of the conflict?

In other words, creativity sometimes means changing the time order. This comes with a built-in guarantee that it is not too creative because the elements are already known. And what can be done in time can also be done in space. Look at where the kitchen is located today relative to a century ago when it was on the periphery of the apartment or house, by the backyard. Now it is quite frequently in the centre, the walls are partly removed (like the housemaid). She/he who prepares the food can join in in everything and sees everything. Creative.

(3) *Identify shared axioms of faith*. This is a very effective method, but not always easily practised if one does not know what could be located 'underneath'. Imagine that all parties in a conflict are suffering from the CGT syndrome and that God for one is Satan for the other so that those who see themselves as chosen by God are seen by the others as the instruments of Satan. The prognosis is poor. But there is the possibility of taking the bull by the horns by simply sensitising them to their superstition, the nonsense they have in common. All will protest that it's only the other side that is superstitious, but for us it's not superstition but truth!

A good playwright could communicate this to both sides better than anybody else by using it as a theme for a play. But those who know about such things don't usually write plays, and those who write plays touching on politics know too little about politics, particularly world politics. They may be too fascinated with the characters, the persons, meaning with the micro-level.

The DMA syndrome can sometimes be handled by pointing out that:

- In this conflict we are dealing with (much) more than two parties.
- Other thinks that you are evil and it is your task to convince them that this is not the case after you have asked yourself

what Other will have to do to convince you that they are not born permanently evil.

- There are similar situations that did not necessarily end with Armageddon.

DMA as a bedrock faith has to be shaken. That's not easy when believed so single-mindedly as hard-line Marxists once did. Of course, there are elements of class struggle in most conflicts. But there can also be gender and generation struggle, and nation and state struggle, in many of them. The true believer is the one who has built his image of the world around only one such factor, and then sees everything in the light of his single-factor theory. We can see it very clearly in the simplified Western image of the conflicts in and around Yugoslavia. Those who believe in DMA seize on a single-factor theory, 'Milosevic'. They enjoy it, and whoever 'takes a single-factor theory from an average person will take happiness away from him at the same time', like the division of the world into two parties, bourgeoisie and proletariat, locked in a deadly embrace that leads inevitably to the Armageddon of the world revolution. And after that: heaven on earth. Pure DMA – straight from the Abrahamitic religions.

DIALOGUE

Much can be said here, and much has already been said throughout the book. Let us first indicate a way of organising the dialogue.

We have often talked about diagnosis, prognosis and therapy as ways of relating to a conflict that refuses to go away. The diagnosis is descriptive, based on data, on something that has already taken place – in other words, in the past. The prognosis is also descriptive, but with a jump into the future, just as diagnosis takes the risk of jumping into the deep, from a surface symptom to something deeper, the disease. Both diagnosis and prognosis need theory to take that jump. And they are often controversial.

Therapy is different. It is also future-oriented, like prognosis, but normative, prescriptive. It does not stop at what is going to happen, but focuses on what has to be done. Therapy can be left to the person himself. We shy away from the word 'patient' because that assigns a role to the person, and in English it also has the connotation of having to be patient. Why should a patient be patient, we may ask? Whether we are dealing with efforts to bring about peace or health we can only hope that peace workers and health workers have a sound theory for what they are doing, and that they are not only removing symptoms like surface violence or fever, but are relentlessly pursuing peace and health.

The analytically trained person will immediately see, and before that feel, that something is missing: the normative, applied to the past. It is too late to do anything now. But it is never too late to ask what could have been done in order for what happened not to have taken place: therapy of the past, as a thought experiment, in other words.

Dialogue is based on questioning. But it can take some time to get the other party to become questioning. His inner mood may call forth the exclamation mark 'That's the most stupid thing I've ever heard!' 'Only someone who doesn't live here could ever think of asking something like that!'

So there is a tendency to skirt round the 'hot porridge'. Sooner or later one has to come to the party's own diagnosis of the 'situation' and what he thinks the other parties' diagnoses look like. But it might be wiser to start with the therapy of the past, asking something like 'When did this go wrong, and what could/should have been done at the time?' Experience shows that this type of conversation runs relatively smoothly. The past is less threatening than what is unfolding before one's eyes. Blame will usually be attributed to somebody else. But there may be a high level of consensus about what should have been done, like NATO support from the air for the UN troops in Srebrenica (there was no such thing).

From 'past-normative' we can proceed to the opposite, 'future-descriptive', in other words, to prognosis. 'And how do you think this is going to develop further, as what one ought to have done wasn't done?' A gesticulation, 'Who knows?' All of this is now anchored in the confrontation they have already had with themselves between what happened and what could have been done, and with possible sins of omission.

The time has come to jump straight into the hot porridge, 'past-descriptive', diagnosis; 'And what is underlying all of this?' And after that straight to the centre, 'normative-future': 'What can be done about it?'

The method behind the 40 conflicts is a dialectic between past and future, between the descriptive and the normative. The dialogue and its parties are thrown back and forth between these two poles. The agenda has a built-in guarantee that most relevant aspects are going to be covered. Take your time, be sure that each theme has more or less been exhausted before you move on to the next. But you can take a second round: 'Shall we return to the first question about what could have been done, in the light of what has now been said?'

Then we come to transcendence, transformation and to the creative element. The four points above generally lead to reformulations of some well-known positions. At this point the basic diagram might be useful. The recommendation is to have paper and a pen that writes broadly and clearly to hand, but not naggingly available. 'How does one generally resolve conflicts?' is a good opening remark.

The conflict worker then has to smuggle in some teaching, without making it look like that, and stimulate creativity. One way is: 'What we often find is two or a few extreme positions, so extreme that they can be sustained, or obtained, only through violence. If they are the only outcomes, the conflict is destined to be violent. In other words, we have to find something else and better which can be accepted by both or all of them. Can the little diagram be useful in this conflict?'

In general, the going is smooth from this point on, but what are needed are good bits of information and ideas, playing on identity and isomorphism.

The high point of the dialogue will come when all four agenda points are related to each other, that is therapy of the past with diagnosis of the past with prognosis of the future with therapy of the future, particularly relating the latter two.

The conflict worker has to learn all this by heart. Note-taking is not a good idea unless the conflict parties agree wholeheartedly to it, and under no circumstance use just a tape recorder, and definitely have no researchers there collecting data. Remember, this is a conversation. The relation between the two future perspectives can be extremely sensitive. On the one hand, it is a question of what the party to the conflict says he thinks is going to happen, and what he thinks the second, third and fourth party are expecting, and on the other hand, new ideas about transcendence and transformation. The parties have their doubts, but hope 'that something will come out of all this'. There is still some hope left of winning, or at least that the other party will lose. All the same, new ideas are interesting, even attractive.

There is an old thesis to the effect that if both (let us simplify to two) parties have the same prognosis, then the violent phase of the conflict will soon come to an end and the conflict be resolved. If A thinks that A will win and B also thinks that A will win, why continue?

A bad thesis. B might, for instance, wish to be beaten so that people in doubt can conclude that they fought with great courage against overwhelming odds. In this way, they also deposit a substantial trauma in the world trauma bank, which can be drawn on later. And even if such factors in the deep culture should not be relevant, it may be very difficult to communicate to the other party and admit to oneself that one is heading for defeat. You could try out all the other combinations, but they lead by and large to the same conclusion. The thesis is too rational.

Both parties will always compare their own prognosis with what they think the other party is predicting. At this point the conflict worker should not forget that this is a dialogue, not a debate in which the point is to catch out the other side in a contradiction. The conflict worker will ask questions and one, totally legitimate and important question is: 'Imagine that things turns out the way you think they will; you win. How will the others react? Will they accept your victory or will they start thinking of revenge and revanche?'

In other words, what happens to the prognosis if we bring in the other party's way of experiencing the situation, particularly in the longer run? That is often forgotten. One consequence may be very unpleasant challenges to deeply held convictions.

If both parties reach the conclusion that transcendence is preferable to all other possibilities (continued struggle, withdrawal, compromise), then that is to the good. But it is even better if the transcendence is so attractive that the other four outcomes simply wither away and all attention is concentrated on giving the transcendence content.

All this should ideally come from inner conviction or inner acceptance. Third parties, often big powers and 'realist politicians' are far removed from reality in their 'realism' when they limit themselves to the other two forms of power: punishment and reward. 'If you don't do as I say, then you will be carpet-bombed', or 'If you do as I say, you will get a carpet of gold.' Clearly, a cease-fire can also result from such pressure, but based on the sour taste of fear or the sweetness of bribes, not on inner acceptance. The big power exerts its will, but that is not the same as transforming the conflict so that the parties can live with it non-violently and creatively, in peace.

The conflict worker brings to the dialogue his general conflict knowledge, using identity and isomorphism, and his skills. The conflict parties bring deep specific knowledge about the conflict. In that way they meet as equals. Both have something to give the other.

It all happens *dia logos*, through the word. The language is simple, questioning without examining, in an even and pleasant tone of voice. Try to avoid words of negation: 'no', 'but', 'however'; they invoke a defensive response in the other party. And watch your body language! No expression of boredom by looking at your watch, and don't take on the posture of a teacher by straightening your back, looking diagonally at the party, or aggressively by locking eyes with him and even pointing at him, or leaning your body forward like a predator before its prey. Negative emotions like that should not be expressed in body language. Sit in a relaxed way, leaning back as if in a comfortable saloon/sofa for a chat, legs together, parallel or crossed, one over the other. And watch your dress code: keep it neutral.

To avoid complications dialogues might also preferably be organised among men only, or among women only.

As an example, here is an extract of a real dialogue, between an Indonesian general, IG, and a conflict worker, JG:

JG: Thanks for inviting me to this conversation. Can we talk about the future of Indonesia?

IG: Future!! You're playing with words! Indonesia has no future!

JG: No future?

IG: The communists are everywhere, dividing the country!

JG: Communists? There was a referendum in East Timor with a clear majority for independence. Were they all communists?

IG: Maybe not all of them. Fellow travellers. The communists started down there in Angola and Mozambique, then they came to Lisbon but did not succeed in seizing power. They ended up here.

JG: General, how does the military future of Indonesia look?

IG: Ha! The Americans are coming! The Kennan Plan right after the war: a US fleet in Indonesia controlling South Asia, Southeast Asia and East Asia! The day after East Timor becomes independent, as they call it, the USA will get a military base. Mark my words!

JG: And the alternative?

IG: The security in this archipelago is our, only our, task!

JG: What does Indonesia's economic future look like?

IG: Ha!! Australia is coming! They call it 'peace-keeping'! Oil-keeping is what it is. They want all the oil between Timor and Darwin. The day after 'independence', as they call it, they will be everywhere, drilling for oil. Mark my words!

JG: And the alternative?

IG: All the resources in the archipelago are ours, ours only!

JG: How about the cultural future of Indonesia?

IG: You mean religion? OK, I am a Muslim, but I don't like fundamentalists. We need religion; it makes my soldiers more disciplined. Perhaps me too! – ha ha ha!! And I do not like missionaries imposing their religion on others. The day after East Timor becomes independent, as they call it, the Vatican will be there to 'evangelise'. Mark my words!

JG: And the alternative?

IG: To live together as best we can. Tolerating each other.

JG: How about the political future?

IG: All crumbling, we have no future! First East Timor, then Aceh, the Malakkas, Papua-Irian Jaya, and a couple of others you do not know about, ha! We have lived together for centuries, the same flesh and blood, strong ties, we have married each other. All of that will be torn apart because of some communists and fundamentalists!

JG: And the alternative?

IG: I could weep. We could live together in this archipelago.

JG: How about a federation, each part with its own culture, with open borders and joint foreign, security and finance policy?

IG: Like the Soviet Union? We know what happened there!

JG: That was no federation. The Russians had all the power. Switzerland?

IG: With cuckoo clocks? Ha! But East Timor wants independence?

JG: They could be both free and associated with an Indonesian federation. Like Switzerland or Liechtenstein. With soft borders.

IG: Federation? Associated? Hmmm. Tell me, could you come to my office tomorrow at 8 am? I have some friends we could talk with.

The conflict worker sticks to '?' and keeps calm, not pursuing the moot point about 'communism'. The conflict party opens with '!'. The breakthrough comes when he changes to '?'. At that point real dialogue, mutual search and discovery start. A delightful experience.

NEGOTIATION

Advice like this is also valid for negotiations. The table where the parties meet can take all kinds of shapes. Opposite parties may be located across from each other, with the leaders of the delegations in the middle, on both sides of a long table; possibly with a mediator at the end of the table. Many parties can meet around a round table, which has the advantage that there is no position in the middle or at the end; everybody is equal. In the centre are the neutrals – interpreters and secretaries. For both kinds of table there can be an outside row/circle of advisers, etc.

If there are three, four, five, six parties a triangular, quadrangular, pentagonal or hexagonal table can be used. If the conference is used for negotiation, as is often done in the United Nations and national assemblies, with many parties, then there is usually a podium for the leadership of the conference (president, staff), and a floor for the participants who will be speaking either from their seats or from the rostrum. In addition, there are committee rooms with tables of all kinds of shapes. But the best venue is usually a cafeteria where small tables can be moved, put together, etc. In UN organisations delegates' dull eyes start to shine.

There are other possibilities. TRANSCEND has a position with regard to tables: by and large, avoid them. The dialogue is based on a one-to-one conversation and can best be done with two chairs juxtaposed diagonally to each other. Chair facing chair is an unfortunate symbol of point and counterpoint just like the long table, and chair parallel to chair is simply uncomfortable. Two sofas, at an angle of 90°, with a small table in between for drinks is OK. How the room is furnished is important; there is an architecture to conflict transformation.

Sometimes other people will come into the picture, at the same time. In that case small tables, round, square, long, with seating for four to six, can be arranged in a semi-circle so that everybody can see and listen to what is going on at the centre, and can easily turn round if each table also becomes a dialogue group. In practice, the dialogue group will also become a negotiation group about how the task can be solved. The borderline between seminar and negotiation is transcended. And that is exactly the purpose; a good seminar is a good model.

Let us make a distinction between *soft* and *hard* negotiations. In a very useful textbook about negotiations by Raymond Saner, *The Expert Negotiator*, the tactic of negotiations is summarised under the heading 'Behind enemy lines':

No general or commander will attack a serious adversary head on. That would be foolish to say the least, and probably suicidal.

A much better objective is to attack the undefended flank. The enemy's supply lines are also relatively vulnerable, if we can get to them with our own forces. In the military domain, this task is effected by tactical missiles or the use of paratroopers. Over the longer term, psychological warfare by way of tracts dropped over civilian areas or radio broadcasts has proved highly effective. At the negotiating table, an equivalent function would be exerted by an operation behind the lines if it attacked the other side's supporting groups, or strengthened its opponents. (p. 145)

This is precisely what is at the root of the scepticism in this book about negotiations, apart from the fact that the best that comes out of negotiations is usually what we have called 'a flat compromise', in other words, without that jump upwards into transcendence. The problem is not the author's use of war as a metaphor. It is that this is the correct metaphor for *hard negotiations*. They are a continuation of war by other means. The front lines are called positions, there is fighting over the terrain between them. How much a party is ready to sacrifice and willing to retreat is kept secret. Victory comes to the party whose original position is closest to the result of the negotiation.

Here is another example, from the less useful *The Negotiator's Handbook* (pp. 67–8) – six tactics to make your arguments more effective:

- support your arguments with documentation, preferably printed;
- bring in experts to support your position; the more authoritative, the better;
- avoid using unfounded claims;
- admit weaker aspects of your proposal before the opposite party does so;
- if you can't rebut something that was said, shift the focus to something else;
- choose the right point in time, like an upbeat mood, to close the deal.

A combination of truisms, and small, cheap tricks. Very far from any attempt to come together in order to create a new reality.

A very well-known, and interesting, book about negotiations is *Getting to YES: Negotiating Agreement without Giving in*, by Roger

Fisher and William Ury from the Harvard Negotiation Project. Given Harvard's role as the brain of the superpower USA the book should be read with a curious scepticism. And that is confirmed by two conflict workers on diametrically opposite parts of the globe telling the present author, 'Fisher was here, and promised us money from the US Embassy if we would promise to use only his method, only his book, and to display it publicly.'

Among the case studies the authors use are the negotiations between the USA and Iran in 1980 about the release of 52 diplomats and embassy personnel kept hostages in Tehran by militant students. They present the US position, *release the hostages*, briefly, simply, correctly. But this is followed by a psychological model of what might possibly make a student leader say yes or no. At this point nothing is said about the constant interference on the part of the USA in the internal affairs of Iran, the coup against Mossadegh, the power given to the Shah, the organisation of resistance against Khomeini in the US Embassy, all of this documented in what the embassy personnel were not able to burn, then printed and distributed throughout Iran as protocols. And that material was not about the prestige of student leaders.

As far as we know the 52 diplomats are still bound by secrecy, but the position of the student leaders was easily available and was, by and large, as follows:

- The USA should admit their interventions in internal Iranian affairs.
- The USA should apologise.
- The USA should promise to refrain from anything similar in the future.

Ambitious demands to a superpower, but not very creative.

President Carter, who knew little about Iran, asked the State Department whether there was any truth to these accusations. They probably experienced considerable nervousness in their effort to justify a 'no'.

The USA made an abortive and humiliating intervention in the desert, but in the end the hostages were released against adequate payment so that Ronald Reagan, the incoming president got all the credit, not Jimmy Carter. In other words, any perspective on both sides was lacking. And the USA–Iran conflict continues, as is well known.

What would TRANSCEND have recommended? Release in return for an apology, and a truth and reconciliation commission, as we would have said today. And, if the USA does not apologise, then spread Iran's truth all over the world and release the hostages for humanitarian reasons without demanding anything in return. The world will know what conclusions to draw.

However, what is more serious is the whole theory of negotiation in the book. The basic idea is to take the interests of the parties, rather than their positions, as a point of departure. They add that the deepest interests are the basic needs of human beings. Positions are often *formulated* inflexibly. But basic needs like physical well-being and identity *are* inflexible. If they are insulted or neglected, then the negotiations will produce nothing but common insecurity. If basic needs are satisfied, then the result could be common security. In the interests there is not necessarily more flexibility than in the positions, rather less.

Then they introduce some *theory*: the parties have to justify theoretically that their positions will satisfy their true interests. This kind of exercise, however, plays into the hands of the theoretically more gifted party, and becomes a question of position and counter-position. The other party will not – like a conflict worker in a TRANSCEND dialogue – help all parties formulate their positions as well as possible, but will rather be searching for the weak points in the theory referring positions to interests. Custom-made for somebody from Harvard.

The authors seem to believe that the parties can revise their positions if the theories linking their positions to their interests do not hold water. At this point there seems to be an interesting cultural difference between the USA and continental Europe where 'theory' is concerned.

An American can easily see a theory as a tool; if the theory doesn't work, change tools. But the European, and particularly the German or French, will have a quite different view. To challenge his theory that the positions derive from his interests will easily lead to a theory conflict so strong and so unsolvable that the original positions will be forgotten. All this is very different from taking the positions as a point of departure, loosen them a little, then transcend and transform. The TRANSCEND model is a relaxed, deep and searching conversation. Fisher–Ury's model seems to be that of a trenchant Harvard University seminar.

Another book worth mentioning, perhaps more because of who its author, Edward de Bono, is than for its content, is *Conflicts: A Better Way to Solve Them*. The book is above all a lengthy argument for the subtitle, using his rightly famous *lateral thinking* as the means to arrive at creative solutions. New to the field, he has little or nothing to offer about conflict life cycles that others haven't already said considerably better, generations ago. He has a proposal which is more of an organisational nature: he wants to establish a SITO, a Supranational Independent Thinking Organisation, as a forum where parties to a conflict can have permanent dialogues with each other, on a daily basis, face to face. Well, why not?

He gives an example of his lateral thinking about a particular conflict and, as the saying goes, the proof of the pudding is in the eating. Once again, it is Iran and the hostage crisis. He was asked a direct question by a TV journalist, 'What's your proposal?' a completely justified question to anybody who presents himself as a conflict specialist, and something the peace movement should always prepare very well. If they themselves have nothing to say, then they do not have any right to complain that the media and politicians are so poor where solutions are concerned. So he said:

> [It] seemed to me that the main point in the Iranian students holding the hostages was that this considerably upset the USA. If 'somehow' the USA could signal patience and that it would not be blackmailed in this manner, then there would be little point in holding the hostages. Such a signal would seem very callous and uncaring for the hostages (although it might have secured their earlier release). So I suggested that each hostage would receive $1,000 a day from the US Government as compensation for this unfair imprisonment. Each day a hostage would know that something beneficial had happened and that patience had some reward at least.

With a proposal like this he places himself far outside the field. Like Fisher–Ury he cannot imagine that the students could have a goal, never mind a valid goal. That can be understood without agreeing with them. As a proposal in the lesser conflict between Washington and the hostages themselves the solution is creative. But for the greater conflict between the USA and Iran it is simply ridiculous. And that is the root conflict.

The last example in the same direction is from a book that has much valuable material about communication and some of the best advice about the significance of empathy, and not only intellectual understanding, for communication: Marshall Rosenberg's *Nonviolent Communication*. He refers to a presentation in a mosque in a refugee camp in Bethlehem, for about 170 Muslim Palestinian men. The attitude to Americans was negative, so one man suddenly leapt to his feet and shouted to Rosenberg 'Murderer!' and right after that there was a chorus of a dozen other voices shouting 'Assassin!', 'Child-killer!'

Rosenberg was concentrating on what the man was feeling and what his needs were and said to the one who had called him a murderer:

- Are you angry because you would like my government to use its resources differently?
- Damn right I'm angry! You think we need tear gas made in USA? We need sewers, not your tear gas! We need housing! We need our own country!
- So you're furious and would appreciate some support in improving your living conditions and gaining political independence?
- Do you have any idea what it's like to have lived here 27 years the way I have with my family – children and all? Have you got the faintest idea what that has been like for us?
- It sounds like you are feeling very desperate and you are wondering whether I, or anybody else, can really understand what it is like to be living under these conditions.

In other words, Rosenberg does not take a stand, but translates the violent language of the other to a more non-violent, 'feeling' language.

> Once the gentleman felt satisfied I understood, he was able to hear me as I explained my purpose for being at the camp. An hour later, the same man who had called me a murderer was inviting me to his home for a Ramadan dinner.

And with that the micro-conflict between the two was solved. But how about the macro-, mega-conflict between the USA and Palestine? This was reductionism to the micro-level.

Is there a negotiation concept fully compatible with the TRANSCEND method? Certainly, and that is what is meant by *soft negotiations*. Concretely, it is relatively obvious what it implies: instead of empathic, non-violent, creative dialogues with a conflict worker who tries to make the parties ready for the negotiation table this link in the chain is removed and the parties have dialogues directly with each other.

The dialogue can still be between two, one from each party, three if there are three parties, under four, six eyes in order to avoid too much theatre effect. They will try to get under the skin of each other and themselves in a questioning way, not in the drilling way of a debate.

If each delegation has, say, five members then one way of starting would be with five dialogue pairs, perhaps organised in such a way that they meet their counterpart: president with president, assistant with assistant, foreign minister with foreign minister. The next day they can continue, or they can change partners so that all of them can dance their dialogues with each other, in all 25 pairs. At the end the outcomes from all this brainstorming has to be pulled together. The many small creeks have to become a river. And for that to happen they may need a conflict worker.

If there are many parties, then round tables or some other shape without a fixed centre and a clear periphery are recommended. And if time is limited, then several tables can be active at the same time, each one for 'opposite numbers', and each table with the same theme and a limited time frame. Each table will then elect a rapporteur who will make a presentation to everybody.

The ideal setting for all these tables would be something like a banqueting room. The order in which the tables are called could be random, or at least different each time so that the same table does not always get the advantage or disadvantage associated with being first, middle or last. Start with some general exercises far removed from the concrete conflict, then come closer. At least this is the way TRANSCEND operates.

In other words, there is a sliding transition from a TRANSCEND seminar, where the purpose is to learn about conflict transformation, to seminars with a strong element of negotiation. 'We thought we had come here to learn, and discovered at the end of the week that we actually had negotiated ourselves towards some quite good proposals for the conflicts of the region, and at the same time benefited from each other's comments and from those of the course directors' is a typical comment. This can often best be done if the theme is not 'the conflicts in and around Afghanistan' but 'the future of Afghanistan'. For the Middle East this works better when groups of journalists from Israel, Palestine, Jordan and Egypt discuss 'the Middle East I would like to live in' rather than 'the Middle East conflict' (this is what TRANSCEND did in June 2000). Try to talk constructively about the future, not destructively about the past, particularly when the pain of the conflicts is experienced deep in the soul. Sooner or later the past has to be attended to, however.

The big question is whether participants in negotiations at a high level are willing, and if willing are able, to do anything like this.

Some of them may find it beneath their dignity, like playing in a sandpit. They are ready to enact the most antiquated diplomatic rituals where style of speaking, dressing, eating and drinking are concerned, but feel that 'the name of the game is to play hardball', 'We are here to win the negotiations, not to have an excursion into the land of dreams. We know what this is all about, it's his interests or mine.' It is precisely because of such attitudes that a preparatory dialogue with a conflict worker is recommended.

Can they change gear from trying to convince to mutual enrichment, from debate to dialogue, from exclamation mark to question mark, from the imperative to the subjunctive? Of course, individually they can, we are talking about highly intelligent, clever people. But are they as a group able to proceed from antagonism to cooperation? With witnesses present? That's problematic.

The reader will have understood by now that the proposals in these pages are efforts to transcend the contradiction between dialogue and negotiation. The two extreme positions are *dialogue with one party at a time* and *hard negotiations in order to win*. And the transcendence is to have direct dialogues with each other, rather than debating, in order to develop ideas and not to win; not only in pairs, but in groups. The dialogue is the key element. It is close to a good university seminar and a good conversation. Diplomats are civilised, bourgeois human beings, so both should be familiar. The problem might be the instruction they carry at the back of their minds from the ministry back home: Protect our national interests! That relationship is vertical, often expressed in a secret code, not eye to eye. To have a dialogue with the ministry about these instructions, high-status members in the delegations are needed.

Soft negotiations are better than hard ones. But aren't hard negotiations preferable to war? Yes, words can be very hard, insulting, but they are not lethal. The problem is rather that when negotiations are taking place people are filled with false expectations. A good reason why the doors are usually closed is because what happens behind them often cannot stand the light of the day. The problem is not necessarily that the negotiators are carried away by their emotions, but rather that they sometimes are too cold to have emotions at all, and are even proud of it. Sometimes there might even be an advantage to emotions finding expression as they often do in a court case: 'He broke down', 'She started crying'.

The problem is often intellectual. They are clumsy. They are short on techniques to structure the problems, the contradictions. They are not in possession of the basic facts. And they suffer from an absolute deficit of empathy and creativity whereas they are reasonably non-violent around a table. The prize will easily go to the party that is best prepared. And the name of that party in international negotiations is often the USA. This does not mean that the USA necessarily has the best ideas, but that others must try to get their act together.

Sunday: The Transcend Method
– An Overview

Two old ladies have been hit by a lorry at a village crossroads. The driver was under pressure to meet a deadline, and the ladies wanted what everybody wants, to live their lives unmolested. Conflict language does not express the depth of the tragedy. But it serves to enable us to ask a question, how do we relate to this problem?

There are three approaches:

1. An ambulance is called, the two ladies die on the way to hospital, court case, sentence and punishment, better warning signs at the intersection.
2. A road engineer is called, a bridge for pedestrians, a roundabout, speed bumps, possibly a bypass.
3. A system debate is called for, with hard critique of capitalism in general and cars in particular, of the pressure to buy, pressure to meet deadlines, time pressure in general.

How does TRANSCEND relate to this kind of situation? The second alternative would be our preferred choice. The first answer does not solve any conflict, it only tidies up after a violent meta-conflict. The third alternative is good if it leads to concrete ideas that can be realised within a reasonable time frame. But the second proposal has the advantage that it can be done here and now in a sustainable way if it is accepted by the parties to the conflict, and that means not only drivers and pedestrians, but also public agencies and political parties. Modern society is poor in institutions that make such parties relate to each other in a direct dialogue; indirect approaches are preferred.

The bridge is literally speaking a good transcendence. But the roundabout is more creative. Traffic speed is reduced, it is friendlier to the environment by reducing idling of the engine, it is less expensive than traffic lights and gives vehicles more than the three possibilities in traditional intersections. The roundabout can also be made aesthetic, as in France. The art of engineering.

TRANSCEND is liberal in the sense of encouraging small steps; Marxist in the sense of building on transcendence and the dialectics of contradiction; and Buddhist in the sense of having basic human needs as the fundamental guide. As anybody can ascertain from reading this book the proposals even for solving the mega-conflicts can be creative, but hardly revolutionary in the conventional sense.

Behind that there is a basic attitude. The world is crying out for change and proposals exist to solve many problems. But proposals can also create problems of their own. We know what we have, not what we will get. Hence, it is better to proceed carefully with small steps than with big, time-consuming projects exposing large parts of the world to something that has never been tested on a more modest scale. Why? Because we may be wrong.

For that reason to say of an agreement that it has been etched in steel or hewn in stone is not a compliment. *Of a good agreement we should request that it is reversible, that it can be undone.* Only do what you can undo. It is possible to exit from a confederation after reasonable notice has been given. A federation should also be made in such a way that exits are permitted. Of course, the hope is that a transcendence will be so successful that it becomes a new social reality, which in turn produces its own contradictions which then can be transcended, and so on. History, in other words. But if it is not successful, then there should be a road back to the point of departure, not only roads pointing in alternative directions.

Values are fundamental; they set the course. But theory is also needed as a map of uncharted territory. And data are indispensable in order to know where we are. All true research is action research. All true politics is an experiment where value- and theory-driven action will be confronted with data on behalf of humanity. Such research takes place in a triangle between values, theory and data, adjusting them to each other.

To some of these proposals the reader may have shaken his head and said or thought something like 'OK, but this will never work.' Wise heads said exactly that in connection with Ecuador–Peru and Cold War I, and all the other cases for that matter. But that rests on a misunderstanding. There is no thesis that everything will work as long as it is located along the peace diagonal. The thesis is that if something works, then that is where the solution will be found. That a conflict needs time for transformation is obvious. The deeper the conflict is located in basic needs, the more solid are its roots. The conflict worker is sowing seeds of transcendence for conflict transformation, ideas that can grow high at the side of the conflict and in the end overshadow it.

Ideas are like seeds. They have to relate to the ideal world of the parties and if possible emerge from those worlds, with the conflict worker as facilitator. Sometimes he can make a synthesis, which is an extrapolation from their ideal worlds, and play that synthesis back to them. In this work the seeds have to be watered regularly – and that is where peace journalism and peace education come in. If a creative idea based on empathy is to be carried out in a non-violent way, then it has to be made available in public space. The idea must benefit from public debate. There is no faith here in ideas reached behind closed doors, which remain closed above all to hide the fact that no good ideas have emerged. In order for good ideas to emerge in public space, in the media, in assembly halls, around dining tables they have to be formulated and marketed. In order to clothe them with words somebody has to pronounce those words. And those people have to be prepared for Schopenhauer's saying that whoever has a new thought will first be ridiculed, then persecuted, until in the end somebody says, 'That has always been my conviction.' This is a burden one has to be prepared to take on. In fact, it's an easy burden. Including silence. Schopenhauer forgot that.

In this book a number of nasty things have been said about the number 2. The book is about turning one's back on the two extremists, choking them with a compromise, but preferably transcending them, transforming them. But the diagram itself has two axes, and the conflict is often formulated as being between two parties.

More complex conflicts and their transformation are outside the framework of this book, however. But the book is not two-dimensional even if the point of departure usually is two parties. We start with two also because so many others in the world do so. We are easily captivated by the clear speech of strong parties: this is a struggle over 'full independence' as opposed to 'living in slavery'. '*Patria o muerte!*' 'Better dead than red!' – or vice versa, some people said during the Cold War. It's all very clear.

Our task is to loosen up, to place the extremists in the diagram and then find creative answers to the three points standing there, whispering or shouting Who am I? What happens next, as we have seen many times, for instance in Northern Ireland, is that behind each point on the peace diagonal there are more or less conscious attitudes, and behind these attitudes there are parties that can be mobilised if they could be given a little more faith that what they are halfway thinking, halfway saying is sustainable and could be accepted by most people given some hard work.

The diagram accommodates at least five answers to Who am I?, not two. The objection may be that the book has relegated the extremists to a corner without giving them sufficient recognition for being the first to bring the conflict out in the open and into the consciousness of the public. The conflict is often latent, on a back burner. The extremists enter the arena as carriers of clear goals and make the conflict public. The problem is that violence easily follows in their wake, and with violence no sustainable solution. In other words, transcendence and transformation are called for. And that demands real conflict work beyond what extremists can offer.

Is the book too optimistic? Well, what is wrong with the optimist's moral heart and idealism, provided there is also some realism somewhere in the brain? What is needed is a time perspective, but not too long. What is needed is creativity, but not too much.

The ideologist who wants to transcend and transform everything and everybody except himself is not a conflict worker.

The researcher who explores reality and presents beautifully in a book, perhaps even in a straitjacket referred to as social science laws and regularities, is not a part of conflict work either. This straitjacket has a name in the philosophy of science, it is referred to as *positivism*. In practice, this means that everything that might have happened in the past, and everything qualitatively new that could happen in the future apart from continuation of the past and past trends, is beyond the active concern of the researcher.

But in conflict work the task is exactly to create new realities. For this a sharp vision is needed, as well as a long vision for the longer run, but not television (the last remark being directed against how TV across the world fails to do a good job for peace by peaceful means). The researcher has to descend from the ivory tower, and perhaps the ideologist should enter the tower. The researcher in 'international relations', a misnomer for 'interstate relations', will be astonished to see how many parties there are, or can be created, in this world. Only a few of them are states, many of them are nations. Positivistic analysis of the state system is a poor guide. New actors have to be created.

Nevertheless, what has been proposed may not work at all! In all probability this is because we have not been able to catch the whole conflict formation. Thus, one or more of the parties may have the tension of the conflict, and the *frisson* of excitement of violence, as a goal in itself. Usually we can find good explanations in deep cultures and/or in the deep structure as indicated above. For that more expertise is needed, and that can be learned.

In principle, yes. But look at the Danish *Morgenavisen-Jyllandposten*. 19 January 2002: 'The Police Arming for EU Summits'. Denmark had the EU presidency for the second half of the year from 1 July 2002, so we are talking of eleven or twelve meetings. They expected violent demonstrations. Four thousand police officers had to be trained. Cars, radio and other equipment had to be bought at a cost of 40 million kroner, 'depending on the perceived threat'. Lawyers, courts and prisons had to be made ready. The total expenditure was estimated at 125 million kroner.

Why so much violence at the World Bank–IMF–WTO summits, the G8 and EU, and not at the big UN conferences? Because everything is held behind closed doors, with elites listening only to each other.

What are the parties' goals? Government elites want to work in peace and quiet, which is perfectly legitimate. But the people they govern want to be listened to and participate in decisions concerning themselves. Known as democracy, this is also legitimate.

How can we bridge this gap? This is exactly what the UN has done so well since the environment conference in Stockholm 1972, by having an alternative forum for the world civil society running in parallel to the governmental conference, with the same agenda. There has to be communication between the two conferences, and that is usually the task of journalists. But there will also always be somebody with access to both who can have a mediating function.

Both/and would have saved 125 million kroner. Add to that the income to Copenhagen from thousands of NGO people. The city could put tents at their disposal in its excellent parks and some security guards. This is the way mature people would handle a situation like this. But somewhere in the World Bank, etc. there is a mental block against learning from the UN, which also has economy and livelihood on its agenda. The UN has contributed a lot to the development of democracy with its open forums. But the World Bank–IMF–WTO–G8–EU are still living in a state of feudalism.

Another case, *Washington Post/Japan Times* 1 November 1999.

Protestant and Catholic Christianity have been struggling for a long time with the problem that arose when Martin Luther presented his 95 theses on 31 October 1517. They are still powerful and make good reading.

A key point was the theory of salvation by the grace of God. Simply put, the Catholics claimed that the road to salvation passed through faith and good works, whereas the Protestants (Lutherans) believed in salvation through faith alone, renewed daily. We are talking here about eternity in heaven so the entrance ticket is important. The doctrine was hammered out in detail in Augsburg in 1530. The two Christianities did not budge whereas the third, Orthodoxy, emphasised the grace of God. Mutual hatred found its expression in 30 years of cruel war, from 1618 to 1648.

After 30 years of negotiation, 482 years later, on 31 October 1999 in Augsburg, the two Christianities came together:

> Together we confess: By grace alone, in faith in Christ's saving work and not because of any merit on our part, we are accepted by God and receive the Holy Spirit, who renews our hearts while equipping and calling us to good works.

A long and not very forceful sentence, redolent of compromise through negotiation. In addition a one-way drive from faith via grace to good works, possibly indicative of a Lutheran bias.

A TRANSCEND analysis would have noticed that neither/nor, negative transcendence, had prevailed through secularisation and the growth of other religions in Europe – Islam and Buddhism. Enlightenment was also inspired by the cruelty of both Christianities in 1618–48.

Is there a both/and? Perhaps, if we look at *outer* action and *inner* faith from above, through God's eyes, as two sides of the same person: Through works based on faith, and faith reinforced through works, we find salvation by the grace of God.

Simpler, but possibly too symmetrical. And yet there's a breakthrough. Like Niels Bohr's 'Is light a wave or a particle? Answer: both/and!, sometimes referred to as 'wavicle'.

However, these formulations are not so epoch-making that 482 years were needed to find them. One explanation is, of course, that the conflict had deeper roots than theological formulations, way down in the economic and political deep structures of the Rhine/North and East Sea against the Mediterranean, and Northern Europe against the Habsburgs/Roman Catholic Empire.

The theological conflict was about being right in the interpretation of God's will. The conflict dissolves through a both/and that preserves both views, but sees them as incomplete insights. But this exercise is only interesting if both/and is more than the sum of the parts. The theological and physical examples serve to remind us that we easily become obsessed with one side of an issue, like the 'inner' or the 'outer', and should learn to look at the issue from above. Be a little god, the creator of humans and of light, to whom the division between the outer and inner human being and between the wave and particle nature of light, are details in the totality of Humans and Light.

So this was the Sunday meditation over all 40 conflicts explored in this book. Have a look at the table of contents and check how both/and and sometimes neither/nor capture a totality beyond the details that caught the imagination of the parties.

Sunday, 6 April 2003 marked the start of the massive US/UK attack to conquer Iraq and control its oil and regime. Kurdish autonomy and Israel/Palestine were also in the frame. TRANSCEND stands for a Middle East restructured through a CSCME, a Conference for Security and Cooperation in the Middle East. A federation for Iraq, Kurdish autonomy in parts of Turkey–Syria–Iraq–Iran, with a confederation of these autonomies. and a Middle East Community of Syria–Lebanon–Israel–Palestine–Jordan–Egypt could be among possible outcomes. But that demands a holistic view often found in world civil society and only rarely in governments. And last but not least a USA which respects international law.

Finally, an overview of the TRANSCEND method for peace by peaceful means. The method is being created, it is not a ready-made product. But here are some basic features from ten years' experience.

Violence has a normal history: passing through untransformed conflict and polarisation. Prior to violence there is usually a polarisation with dehumanisation of the possible antagonists. If in addition there is armament, physical and/or verbal, then we can talk about a cold war, and use that term at the micro- and meso-levels. Prior to that there is usually an unsolved, untransformed conflict somewhere, festering.

Violence has a normal future: more violence. 'Violence breeds violence' is one of the most reliable predictors we know. In other words, the problem is how to break that regularity. In the wake of violence there is not only the desire of the victim for revenge and revanche back to the conflict, with a totally different outcome, there is also the desire of the victor for more victories: it tasted so sweet that addiction is just around the corner.

From this the major programmes of TRANSCEND flow easily:

- *Conflict transformation*, to loosen up the conflicts.

- *Peace building*, against polarisation and dehumanisation in attitude and behaviour.
- *Peace keeping*, to dampen the violence with soft methods.
- *Reconciliation*, healing and closure to break the vicious circle of violence.

In addition there are support programmes such as peace journalism and peace pedagogy in order to enable the population to enter through dialogue about peace proposals and related issues. And all of this acted out in the tense field between contradiction, behaviour and attitude, with deep culture, deep behaviour and deep structure in the deeper layers of the soul, the body and society.

We think it is exciting and that everybody can participate. Take a look at www.transcend.org and start for yourself. Help yourself, steal as much as you want!

One brief but important final remark. Not all incompatibilities and contradictions have to be transcended, dissolved and solved. Mathematics is obsessively inimical to contradictions. Two incompatible theses are a signal that something has gone wrong, but as in the Möbius strip, are also a challenge to transcend by discovering and inventing a new mathematics.

But what about the third possibility: *with this contradiction you can live, continue working towards transcendence, but don't become a victim of facile answers.*

Thus, how can an omnipresent, omniscient, omnipotent and loving God permit so much evil in the world? One possible answer would be to deny one or more of these four properties of God, another to seek a deeper meaning compatible with these properties. Maybe God wants to punish us? Teach us something? Or maybe it was all Satan's work?

I feel more at home with a Buddhist monk's way of putting the problem:

You are right that there is a contradiction between two theses in Buddhism: 'You have no eternal, permanent soul', and 'You will be reborn after death.' But you can live with that contradiction. Continue searching for transcendence, but do not become the prey of any easy answer. You can deny the first thesis, in that case you will feel comfortable with Christian/Muslim rebirth, up in Heaven, or down in Hell. You can deny the second thesis, and you end up as an atheist. Find something better, come back again in 20 years...

I am reborn in my children, I am reborn in the products of my work, I am reborn in the memory I leave behind, I am reborn in the inspiration I try to give to other human beings. We can build our lives around all four. But perhaps attention should be focused on the circumstance that rebirth can be at a higher level or a lower level. Our task as human beings is to be reborn at a higher level. Good conflict work is aiming precisely at that.

And that brings us to the end of the road. The seventh day is also a good day to rest for those who have come this far. Tomorrow you start, more conscious about what can be done with conflicts.

Further Reading

By Johan Galtung:

There Are Alternatives! Four Roads to Peace and Security. Nottingham: Spokesman Press, 1984 (available in seven languages).

Gandhi's Politiske Etikk, (With Arne Næss) Oslo: Tanum, 1955, Pax, 1986.

Methodology and Development. Essays in Methodology. Volume III. Copenhagen: Ejlers, 1988, chapter 2 on dialogue theory.

Peace by Peaceful Means. London, New York, New Delhi: Sage, 1996.

Conflict Transformation by Peaceful Means, Geneva: UN, 1998.

Conflict Transformation by Peaceful Means, Geneva: UN, 2000.

Searching for Peace: The Road to TRANSCEND, (With Kai-Frithjof Brand-Jacobsen) London: Pluto Press, second edition, 2002.

By others:

Edward de Bono, The Use of Lateral Thinking, London: Penguin, 1971.

Edward de Bono, Conflicts, A Better Way to Solve Them, London: Penguin, 1985 (quote from p. 89).

Julius Fast, Body Language, New York: PocketBooks, 1971.

Roger Fisher and William Ury, Getting to YES: Negotiating Agreement without Giving in, New York: Penguin, 1991 (quote from pp. 44–8).

George Fuller, The Negotiator's Handbook, Paramus NJ: Prentice Hall, 1991 (quote from pp. 67–8).

Arne Næss, Livsfilosofi: Et personlig bidrag om følelser og fornuft, Oslo: Universitetsforlaget, 1998.

Arne Næss, Gandhi and Group Conflict, Oslo: Universitetsforlaget, 1974.

Marshall B. Rosenberg, Nonviolent Communication: A Language of Compassion, Del Mar, CA: Puddle Dancer Press, 1999 (quote from pp. 11–12).

Raymond Saner, The Expert Negotiator, Haag: Kluwer Law International, 1997 (quote from p. 145).